HOW SCRUTABLE ARE THE JAPANESE!

This book was originally written in Japanese ! Japanese linguist for Japanese English-language learners. It was subsequently translated into English, with some alterations for Japanese-language learners and those who teach English to Japanese, because it gives both the reason why the Japanese are so bad at learning English as well as providing the most effective way of teaching English to the Japanese. It also elucidates certain Japanese national characteristics, which have for a long time been enshrined in mystery.

ABOUT THE AUTHOR

Eiichi Kawata was born in 1950, in Saitama Prefecture, Japan. He hardly spoke any English until he went to England at the age of twenty-three. Four years later, he was able to embark upon a postgraduate course to study International Economic Law at the University of London. While he was a postgraduate student, he mixed with various foreign students and developed an excellent listening ability. Earning a reputation for being able to speak English as well as a native English speaker, he established 'the Kawata Method of Learning English Conversation' by clearly demonstrating how to pronounce 'the actual sound of R as it is heard in words'.

After finishing his dissertation in International Economic Law at London University, he studied French at Grenoble University, France. By obtaining a proficiency certificate in French in less than a year he proved his remarkable talent for languages. Not only in the field of languages but through his relations with many different nationalities, Eiichi Kawata also became thoroughly acquainted with the national characteristics of many other countries and nurtured a real international understanding.

Returning home, he established Fukaya Foreign Languages Institute in Fukaya, Saitama Prefecture, which in 2002, changed its name to The Research Institute of Linguistic Strategies (TRILS). At the present time Eiichi Kawata is also internationally active as a Rotarian.

How Scrutable are the Japanese!

◇

LEARN HOW TO TEACH ENGLISH
TO THE JAPANESE
AND
HOW TO SPEAK JAPANESE
AT THE SAME TIME!

◇

Eiichi Kawata

RENAISSANCE BOOKS

HOW SCRUTABLE ARE THE JAPANESE!
LEARN HOW TO TEACH ENGLISH TO THE JAPANESE AND HOW TO SPEAK
JAPANESE AT THE SAME TIME!

First published 2005 by The Research Institute of Linguistic Strategies
11-7 Fukaya-cho, Fukaya-shi
Saitama-ken
Japan 366-0825

Second edition 2008

Designed and produced by
Renaissance Books, England

Printed in England

ISBN 978-1-898823-50-6

British Library Cataloguing in Publication Data
A CIP catalogue entry for this book is available
from the British Library

Contents

☐ Preface

IN MARCH 2002, I had an opportunity to give a talk at the Oxford Union (Oxford University). The talk was entitled, 'How scrutable are the Japanese? Who can teach them English?' The audience gathered there were mainly native English-speaking teachers of the English language rather than students.

Among other things, I put to them quite bluntly that the reason why the Japanese are incapable of speaking English properly is because native English teachers are not teaching English correctly to the Japanese. In particular, 'the actual sound of "R" as it is heard in words', which does not exist in Japanese and is indispensable for the Japanese to aquire in order to master conversational English, is not taught properly by the native English speaker. Or rather, native English speakers cannot teach it to the Japanese because the teachers themselves have never been taught how to pronounce the sound on its own.

During the post-speech question-time at the Oxford Union, all the participants agreed and said, as if in chorus, that the Education, Science and Technology Ministry of Japan should change 'ra ri ru re ro' into 'la li lu le lo' in the Romanized script of the Japanese language. Thus, the central thesis of the Kawata Method was proven valid in Oxford.

Returning home from England, I wrote to the Education, Science and Technology Ministry about my lecture at the Oxford Union and suggested that 'ra ri ru re ro' should be changed at once into 'la li lu le lo' in the Romanized script. Also, I boldly suggested, regarding the reforms of the Japanese English Education System, that the Kawata Method of learning and teaching English should be used in schools across the nation.

☐ Introduction

THIS BOOK WAS originally written in Japanese by a Japanese linguist for Japanese English learners entitled *Because you are Japanese, you've got to be able to speak English well!* It was translated into English with some alterations for Japanese language learners and those who teach English to the Japanese, because it gives both the reason why the Japanese are so bad at learning English as well as providing the most effective way of teaching English to the Japanese. It also elucidates the Japanese national characteristics, which have for a long time been enshrined in mystery.

In writing a book on English conversation, I looked into the question of 'the sound of R', which is the biggest stumbling block for the Japanese to master English. Although every phonetic diagram for the letter R in all the pronunciation exercise books I knew showed that the tip of the tongue did not touch the ceiling of the mouth to create the sound, I realized that I could not communicate with the English if I strictly pronounced the letter R in words according to the diagram. Accordingly, I arranged interviews with many native English speakers about this sound R.

Surprisingly, most of the English people I interviewed actually did not realize precisely what was happening with their tongue. Or rather, they simply took how they were speaking for granted. Therefore, when I pointed it out to them they were all surprised. In the process of my investigation I came to realize that there were two R sounds in English. One is the ordinary R sound in the English alphabet which is created by keeping the tongue flatly resting on the bottom of the mouth, and the other R sound, which can be termed 'the actual sound of R as it is heard in words'. Curiously, this is the very R sound which prevents the Japanese from becoming fluent speakers of English!

Also, as I interviewed the native English speakers it gradually became clearer why the Japanese were unable to acquire 'the actual sound of R as it is heard in words'. That is to say, despite the native speakers being able to pronounce the sound in words, because they were not taught at school in England how to pronounce the sound on its own, they are unable to teach it to the Japanese.

The fact that the native English teachers cannot teach the actual sound of R as it is heard in words on its own to the Japanese has had a negative impact on the Romanized script in Japan, especially the Hepburn System of Romanized script, which was introduced by the American linguist, Curtis Hepburn, almost one hundred and fifty years ago. It was devised initially for the benefit of non-Japanese people to get themselves acquainted with the Japanese language. However, since it was incorporated into the Japanese language, the so-called 'R problem' is being perpetuated.

Currently, within the Japanese education system, the Romanized version of the sounds 'ラ (la) リ (li) ル (lu) レ (le) ロ (lo)' which occur in Japanese are being taught as 'ra ri ru re ro' according to the Hepburn System. Having no such sound as 'the actual sound of R as it is heard in English words' in their language, and as they cannot even recognize the actual existence of the sound itself, it is virtually impossible for the Japanese to pronounce 'ra ri ru re ro'. Consequently, I am advocating that 'ra ri ru re ro' should be changed at once into 'la li lu le lo', which are almost the same as the Japanese pronunciation of 'ラ (la) リ (li) ル (lu) レ (le) ロ (lo)'. Also, at the same time, by using the Kawata R, 'ra ri ru re ro' will have to be taught in contrast to 'la li lu le lo' when they teach children Romaji (Romanized letters) at primary school.

The Kawata Method of Learning English Conversation advocates that the Japanese English education system must start by recognizing and correctly pronouncing those sounds of English which do not exist in Japanese. Above all, 'the actual sound of R as it is heard in words' is the most important one as native English teachers cannot teach it to the Japanese. The Kawata Method clearly shows how this sound on its own should be pronounced and has been duly named 'the Kawata R'.

If you are a native English teacher, once fully acquainted with the Kawata R and the Kawata Method, you will be able to teach English to the Japanese properly and effectively, and if you are a Japanese English learner your English will become intelligible to the authentic English speaker and you will be able to master conversational English.

Now, please do not misunderstand me. Although I argue that a Japanese person is capable of speaking English without being taught by a native teacher, I am not saying we do not need native English-speaking teachers in Japan. What I am trying to say is that, the number of native English speakers in Japan is rather limited, and therefore it is not easy to come in contact with them. However, if native English-speaking teachers are not able to teach the Japanese clearly how to pronounce 'the actual sound of R as it is heard in words on its own', which is an indispensable sound to enable the Japanese to speak English correctly, and if the actual sound of R is learned in Japan, the Japanese might not have to bother to go all the way to England to learn conversational English.

◇

Chapters 8, 9 and 10 are dedicated to Japanese language learners from beginners to advanced. The most significant feature of these chapters is that 'the Kawata System of Romanized script' is used. It is my hope that the system will bring about a new dimension to the learning of the Japanese language for every student.

As already noted, the Hepburn System is still being used in Japan. Its founder made some serious mistakes when he used the letters 'Ff' and 'Rr' in the system. 'The Kawata System' replaces 'Ff' and 'Rr' with 'Hh' and 'Ll'. The reason is clear: F and R (the actual sound of 'R' as it is heard in words) simply do not exist in Japanese.

With this updated 'read-as-it-sounds' lettering of the Kawata System of Romanized script, students should be able to learn proper Japanese and will never encounter ludicrous spellings such as Rondon (London) or rampu (lamp) in their textbooks according to the Hepburn System of Romanized script any more; furthermore, they will be convinced that this is the Japanese language learning material they have been waiting for!

I admit, because of its direct translation into English, the reader might at first find some difficulty in getting used to the style of the language used in this book. I hope, however, that each reader will become much better acquainted with the Japanese national character as well as the Japanese language by the time he or she finishes reading it.

Today, as everyone admits, English is establishing itself as an international lingua franca (common language). There are several reasons why English has become the international lingua franca. It is mainly because of the influence of Great Britain over the world prior to World War II and the impact of the United States since the end of the war up until the present day. However, the main reason why English is so widely spoken in today's world is the fact that English, I think, is easy to learn, especially for Europeans, because it is a mixture of different European languages. The origin of the English language can be traced back to the Western

Germanic languages. Therefore, for the Germans and the Dutch to learn English is almost as easy as learning a dialect in their respective languages. Though to learn the speaking part of English might not be that easy, for these peoples (French, Spaniards, Italians and so on) who speak languages with Latin roots, it is relatively easy to learn as well. In other words, whatever European language they might speak, English is related in some way to their language. For Asians and Africans because of the influence of Great Britain and the US before and after World War II they have naturally adopted English as an international lingua franca.

Why is English, which is an easy language for so many people, thought to be difficult to learn by the Japanese? It is the peculiarity of the Japanese language – that is, as a spoken language: Japanese is very poor in sounds, therefore there are many sounds in English which do not exist in Japanese. It is said that there are three times more sounds in English than in Japanese. The Japanese cannot pronounce all the English sounds hence the reason why their English is not understood worldwide. So, if a Japanese person acquires those English sounds, his/her English will be understood worldwide. Actually, there are only two or three difficult sounds for the Japanese to acquire; but once these are learned speaking English is not that difficult.

◇

There are several reasons as to why I decided to write this book, one of which is that I want the Japanese reader to know that speaking English is not as difficult as they might think, and that a more important thing is not merely to be able to speak English, but 'what you say'. English is simply a means of achieving a cordial understanding. Therefore, I would like Japanese people to have a good command of English, not to be commanded by English, but to have it at their command by enriching their knowledge and education.

On the other hand, I would like the Japanese reader to appreciate the fact that for native English people, speaking English is, to use a metaphor, 'like fighting with real swords', and that they value the spoken language more than purely as a means of achieving a cordial understanding (cf. Chapter 5).

The Japanese middle-aged and senior readers who achieve proficiency in expressing themselves in English after reading this book will be able to use it at once – at work, working abroad or for their holidays.

Having established oneself as a Japanese individual, I would like the young people to go abroad and acquire an international academic career.

I would like them to construct networks of international friends at their universities and post-graduate courses. Such networks will be great assets for them in the future. They would have their reunions, for instance, in Singapore one year and in Paris the following year. Young people will play an increasingly important role in this ever-shrinking world in the twenty-first century.

Acknowledgments
I would like to thank Cos Com Language Service Inc. for granting me permission to reproduce material from their publication *Essential Japanese Verbs*, by Setsu Migita and Y. Yoshimura. I would also like to thank Hodder Headline Plc. for allowing me to refer to their publications *Teach Yourself Japanese*, by H.J. Ballhatchet and S.K. Kaiser, and *Teach Yourself Beginner's Japanese*, by Helen Gilhooly.

My wholehearted thanks go to my mother and my wife, for without the help of these two Japanese ladies it would not have been possible to complete this book in its present form. I am especially grateful to my wife, Miyuki, who has been a great supporter of my linguistic theories, and whose comments reminded me of the most important fundamentals in learning English.

CHAPTER I

☐ Vocal language (English) and visual language (Japanese)

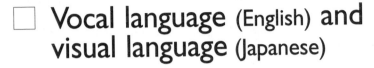

Pronunciation (the sounds of English) first, then rhythm (accent, intonation, etc.) in learning English

ONE OF THE PURPOSES of this book is to present superior English-speaking skills to Japanese English-language learners. Most native Japanese speakers do not pick up these skills naturally and are consequently misunderstood by native English speakers. This can be a very frustrating experience and make the learner wonder if he, or she, will ever be able to master the English language.

The main reason why the Japanese are unable to become fluent English speakers is that they are trying to learn English in the same way as they learn their own language, that is, they are concentrating on the writing and reading parts of the language. Japanese people have to realize that there are differences between English and Japanese, and because of these differences English has to be learnt differently from Japanese. In my view, among the major languages of the world Japanese is uniquely a visual language whereas English is definitely a vocal language. By making themselves fully acquainted with the differences between English and Japanese they will also acknowledge that first they have to acquire the sounds of English which do not exist in Japanese rather than mastering its rhythm (tune, accent, intonation, etc.) in learning English, namely, 'Pronunciation first, then rhythm in becoming a proficient English speaker'. I will explain what I mean by this in due course so that the Japanese English-language learner will know clearly how he/she should approach the language and master it.

- ### The native Japanese speaker can master English even if he/she starts learning it late

(1) My first experiences studying in England

The mothers of prospective English-language students often ask me: At what age should children begin learning English? How early should they start? Based on my experience, I would say that age is not the key issue. Instead, it depends on who is doing the teaching and what form of English is being taught. You can speak English like a native English speaker even if you start learning it after the age of twenty.

My own first exposure to English was during a visit to England when I was almost twenty-three. Taking a year off from university, I was to study English in America as I was considering a career in the diplomatic service. I consulted with my mentor-like professor (whom I shall simply call Professor S.) and he told me: 'Mr Kawata, if you want to study English, do so in England, not America. You will find it a much better place to learn the language. I can find you a language school there where there will be very few other Japanese students; it's better to learn English from the English!'

I was anxious. 'But Professor S., I have never learned any conversational English before. Perhaps it would be better if you were to recommend an English-language school in Tokyo?' 'No,' he replied, 'I am quite serious when I say that it's much better to learn in England. You had better not think about learning in Tokyo because in Japan you are more likely to pick up bad language habits.' So, without ever having studied conversational English, I changed my destination and set out for England. That was in 1973.

When I arrived in England, a kindly Japanese gentleman, whom I had met on the plane, accompanied me from the airport as far as Victoria Station, London. From that point, I was going to travel by myself and I was somewhat apprehensive. At the railway station, I located the ticket office and attempted to buy a ticket for my destination, Ramsgate. Ramsgate is a small seaside town in the county of Kent, not far from the historic cathedral city of Canterbury. On a clear day, you can see the French coast across the English Channel.

I went up to the ticket office and started speaking English with a typical Japanese accent. It went something like this: 'I want a ticket for Lamsgate, please.'

The man in the ticket office looked perplexed. He asked me again and again where I wanted to go. I repeated 'Lamsgate' again and again, and he seemed to be even more confused. I stood there for what seemed a very long time, failing to communicate. I noticed that a long queue was forming behind me and I became very embarrassed. It was clear that there was a communication problem and yet I could only continue to repeat – by this time shouting – 'Lamsgate, please. I want to go to Lamsgate!' – Eventually, he gave me a ticket to Ramsgate.

Later, I understood that the source of the difficulty was that I could not pronounce the English 'r' sound. At that time, I was unaware of this and saw no difference between the 'l' that I used and the 'r' (the actual sound of R as it is heard in words) that was required.

After six months in Ramsgate, I decided to leave and study in Oxford. I had always wanted to go to Oxford and was able to spend six months studying in a language school there. While my teacher, Mr Ian Thompson, was excellent, and while my conversational English improved greatly, it was still far short of perfect. After my stay at Oxford, I returned to my university in Tokyo.

(2) English teaching and my return to England

Back in Japan, I began working as an interpreter and guide for groups of foreign tourists visiting the country. Around this time, I received a telephone call from Mr Iwasaki of Shizuoka, with whom I had studied in the language school in Oxford. He told me that he was inviting Mr Thompson to come over and teach at his language school. He suggested that, if I was interested, I also should join the faculty of his school as an English-language teacher. I agreed, on the condition that I, too, would be able to learn the language from my old teacher Mr Thompson.

During the following twelve months, what I learned from Mr Thompson was to become very meaningful for my life from then on. He taught me a great deal – from learning the alphabet to a point where he encouraged me to come out of my shell and role-play the part of an English person. He taught me technique, but just as importantly he was able to motivate me and to give me a very positive attitude towards my learning and teaching. He never became impatient when I made mistakes, saying: 'A Japanese person can make as many mistakes as he likes when learning English – after all, it is a strange and foreign language so far as he is concerned.'

After working with Mr Thompson, I again resolved to return to Oxford. This time, however, my intent was not to enroll in another language school but rather to gain entry into the very prestigious university itself. However, when I arrived in Oxford, the university expressed no desire to admit me. They advised me quite bluntly that the entrance examinations for foreign students had already taken place and that I would have to reapply the following year. There was nothing to be done.

The university authorities would not concede and I had no other option but to register with a language school in the city and prepare for the entrance examination the following year. And so, from May 1976 until June 1977, I was again studying English in Oxford.

◇

As I was familiar with the routine at the language school, and as I was doing rather well in my studies, I decided to visit the Oxford University Judo Club. The members of the club greeted me warmly and asked me to join them in their practice. After some preparatory work and warm-up exercises, the captain of the Judo Club invited me to a *landoli* – an exercise in Judo, where two opponents try to throw one another. I was anxious. I felt that I had been directly challenged. The atmosphere of the gymnasium seemed to become tense and I felt that everyone was looking at me. Fortunately, I won the competition.

The other members of the club came over to congratulate me and seemed very interested in learning authentic Judo. They asked me if I would teach them some of my skills and I agreed to do so. From that day on, I visited the club on a regular basis and gave lessons to many of the members who quickly became personal friends. Among these pupils was Mr A., who was a lecturer at Oxford University. Some six months later, realizing that I was very anxious to enter his esteemed institution, Mr A. kindly arranged for me to meet with the rector of his college. I was very excited, but I did not really understand the true significance of such a meeting.

The meeting turned out to be an admissions interview. It was conducted informally, and there was no obvious examination. Instead, I chatted for about an hour with this kind and gentle, elderly rector about Britain and Japan. I was concerned that it was my English-language skills that were being examined, but if they were it was to the extent that I was able to converse freely and intelligibly with the rector. He did not test my English *per se*, nor did he formally examine my legal knowledge. I was tense but after a while I began to enjoy the experience and I left the meeting feeling quite optimistic.

Some weeks later, Mr A. gave me a message from the rector stating that he was prepared to accept me into his college's Diploma Course. In the English higher education system, a Graduate Diploma is awarded for university work done between the bachelor and masters levels. I understood that many foreign students were initially placed in the Graduate Diploma programme and, depending upon their success in the end-of-year examinations, are then invited to continue into the master's programme.

I very much wanted to earn a postgraduate credential the following year and now knew that I would be able to enter the Graduate Diploma course at Oxford. However, I thought that it might be possible to obtain a master's degree instead and applied to the University of London. They accepted me directly into their master's programme, which is exactly what I wanted to do. I was undecided and asked my friend Mr A. which of the two schools I should go to – both Oxford and London have an excellent international reputation. He knew that my particular interest was in international law and, after considering the matter, reasoned that my chances of learning more about international law would be greater in the City of London, the heart of the financial world in Europe. Accordingly, he suggested that I should continue my education at the University of London.

(3) My best day in England
Although my English-language skills were by no means perfect, the manner in which I was taught English and the discoveries that I myself made about the language helped me to earn a place in two of England's most selective universities. As I said before, any Japanese learner can acquire the language skills of a native English speaker with the right teacher and with the right methodology. Feeling confident about my English skills, I set off for London University.

Now, let me tell you about a challenge that I encountered in the hall of residence of the University of London, where I stayed for almost three-and-a-half years.

My room was on the fifth floor; in England, by the way, they call the first floor the 'ground floor' and start counting floors after that – first floor, second floor, and so on. My English fifth floor, therefore, would have been called the sixth floor in Japan. On this floor, most of the residents were either postgraduate students or foreign visiting professors. In short, this floor was like a miniature United Nations. Also, on this floor, there were a couple of characters with interesting backgrounds. An Englishman called Mr P. was one of them.

In my second year at the Hall, I was elected as the Floor Representative and dealt with many of the administrative matters of some eighty residents on that floor. Mr P. would often come to visit me. His English was so stylish, and his vocabulary so extensive, that it was often difficult for me to understand him. When I first met him, he would do all of the talking and I was only able to listen. However, it was quite apparent that Mr P. was somewhat idiosyncratic. For instance, he would lose the thread of his reasoning in the middle of a conversation, or become quite blank or absent-minded. Sometimes, when I was speaking to him, he would simply not react at all – as though I was not there. This concerned me somewhat, and I recalled the expression that there's sometimes only a thin line that separates genius from madness.

One day, when Mr P. was talking to me, he noticed that I had become aware of his strangeness. He confided in me that he had been expelled from Oxford University (he used the very idiomatic expression 'I was sent down from Oxford') and that he had spent some time in a hospital for the mentally ill. He suffered, it appeared, from a form of clinical depression. He later showed me an excerpt from an Oxford newspaper that noted he had earned the highest marks in his entrance examination. His revelation was very welcome because I was now able to appreciate his behaviour, which in the past had seemed so idiosyncratic. I sympathized with him and hoped that he would recover completely from his condition. But I also began to admire his spoken English even more than I had in the past. From that day on, I began making a serious effort to improve my English and to expand my vocabulary. It was not easy and I dedicated a great deal of time to the effort.

For Mr P. it was quite natural to speak the way he did. For me after about two years of perseverance, I discovered that there was hardly a word in The Times newspaper that I did not understand. (It is said that most educated English people read this newspaper.) One day, I was speaking to him and used a word that he did not understand! He politely indicated his non-comprehension by saying 'Sorry?' as only the English do. This was the day I had been waiting for. Up until then, I was confident that I had acquired his vocabulary and had been speaking at his level of English. Before that, however, whatever difficult words I used, he had no difficulty in understanding them. Certainly, it might have been a split second, but my English surpassed Mr P.'s English who had scored the highest entrance examination marks at the University of Oxford. Truly, this was one of my best days in England.

● Vocal Language (English) and Visual Language (Japanese)

So, you can really acquire good English, perfectly understandable to the English, even if you start your language studies late. You have to be prepared to work hard, but you also have to have a good teacher and to understand the crucial differences between the English language and the Japanese language. In this section, I will explore these differences and explain why the Japanese are not naturally good at speaking English. Then, I will try to show you how to overcome these problems and how the native Japanese speaker can speak clear, understandable English.

(1) What you must know about English and Japanese

As we know, English is a language that was born in England just as Japanese was born in Japan. The English and the Japanese are both islanders, therefore superficially both nations share some characteristics. For instance, the Japanese as well as the English are fond of talking about the weather, which is a non-committal and inoffensive topic. However, the English were originally nomads on the continent of Europe, moving from one place to another, verbally and skilfully establishing good human relations with people wherever they went, and they became very good at diplomacy. For them, *speaking* became a very important aspect of life and, because of these racial characteristics, English has become a vocal language, a language that has developed more complicated sounds and a wider tonal range than Japanese, distinguishing the meanings of words by sound or by intonation: ban–van, law–raw, and so on.

However, when we talk of Japanese national characteristics, there are two important factors. One of them is that from time immemorial the Japanese have been engaged in agriculture, living in small village communities. The fact that they were an agricultural people tied them to the land and meant that they were not free to move. The second point is that they are islanders and have always been isolated from the rest of the world.

The Japanese have been pursuing their lives in village units throughout history. Whenever natural disasters occurred – like earthquakes, typhoons or famines – they were united and fought against them as a village. Having overcome such natural disasters, they had worked together to get the harvest in and had celebrated it together. They always worked as a village unit. Out of all this, an ideology (absolutism) like 'the village is everything' was born in Japan. Hence, some kind of 'cooperativism'* emerged, in that the Japanese did everything together harmoniously with their neighbours. At the same time, a person or an opinion that might damage the harmony of the village community was virtually eliminated.

---

* 'cooperativism': working together harmoniously with neighbours in the village community for the benefit of the whole village.

In each village, everyone worked silently and diligently. The need for silence was born out of fear because people believed in the old saying that, 'Out of the mouth comes evil'. They knew perfectly well that if they voiced an ill-considered opinion they would be ousted from their village and could face death.

That is to say, once ousted from the village the person would have no place to go since he would be considered a trouble-maker by all the other villages. In Japan, where there is no neighbouring country to escape to, *mulahachibu* (ostracism), was the same as being sentenced to death. From this, it was inevitable that the national character of the Japanese – being taciturn and diligent – was born.

Hence, it seems that the Japanese language has become a visual language, putting more emphasis on writing and reading than on speaking. The introduction of Chinese characters (*kanji*) into Japan, around the third century, established the Japanese language as a visual language.

For instance, observe how this Japanese character ' 大 (*dai*)' means 'big' in English. By adding a dot in the middle of it ' 太 (*hutoi*)', the character changes its meaning to 'thick'. More still, if you put a dot above the character on its right-hand side ' 犬 (*inu*)', it becomes 'dog' in English. In other words, by merely adding a tiny dot to a certain place in a character, or by removing this dot, the whole meaning of the character is changed. In this way, it is possible to distinguish the meaning of one character from another by the sense of vision alone.

Although not as popular as they once were, there are schools called elocution schools in England. They correct your pronunciation and teach you how to speak English well. It is of considerable advantage in England to be able to speak clearly with good diction so that you can command the respect of many people.

On the other hand, in Japan there are numerous calligraphy schools, where the art of writing Japanese is taught because in Japan it is considered a virtue to write Japanese well. This is a good example of how the English and the Japanese view their respective languages differently.

(2) What happens when the Japanese speak English?

I emphasized that English is a vocal language. But there is no general language which is absolutely vocal, it is always in comparison with another language. When English is compared to Japanese, which is very poor in its range of sounds, the contrast is more striking. It is said that English contains three times the number of sounds that are found in Japanese. There are, in fact, several sounds that simply do not exist in Japanese. Because of this, the native Japanese speaker will have to become familiar with those sounds before his or her English is understandable to a competent English speaker. Of particular importance are the English sounds (f), (r), (v), and (th) which represent significant consonants that are not familiar to the Japanese.

For instance, a Japanese person might believe that he or she is saying, 'right, raw and vest' but actually they are pronouncing them as 'light, law and best'. Obviously, this can give rise to considerable confusion – just as when I tried to say 'Ramsgate' but sounded 'Lamsgate'. With this kind of pronunciation you can rest assured that the English will begin looking at you and saying 'Sorry?' and that you will feel more and more embarrassed through lack of language communication skills.

English is a language of the tongue. The Japanese person wanting to speak English must also learn to move the tongue in order to produce these sounds. The sounds 'l' and 'r' in correctly pronounced English are made with the tongue. For the Japanese, this is very difficult to do because they are not used to 'busy tongue movements' when they speak their own language. In particular, the Japanese person must work hard to produce the English 'r' sound. However, if you as a Japanese person manage to become fully acquainted with these English sounds that do not exist in your own language – particularly the 'l' and the 'r' – then your English will be clear and distinct, and understood throughout the world.

● Learning to speak good Standard English

Your goal in speaking English should be to have a clear, Standard English pronunciation with a complete mastery of the difficult sounds that occur in the language but not in Japanese. Unfortunately, while this is an excellent goal to strive for, there are many ways in which you might not reach it. You might become quite satisfied with your own poor English pronunciation, thinking that it is quite understandable, and make no effort to improve. How can this happen? Here are four ways in which you can fail to appreciate that your English needs improvement and that it can, in fact, be improved to become excellent Standard English.

(1) Do not be satisfied if someone who is used to Japlish understands you!

As I have mentioned before, when compared to English, or other European languages, or to Arabic, Japanese is a visual language. Japanese is not rich in sounds, and so while the sound components of these other languages are not found in Japanese, the Japanese sounds are most often present in these other languages. Since the Japanese sounds exist in European languages and Arabic, native speakers of these languages generally do not have a difficult time with the spoken part of Japanese: they are usually relatively quick learners of Japanese. However, they also quickly come to appreciate that sounds like 'f', 'r', 'v', etc. are not present in Japanese and so do not expect to hear Japanese people using these sounds, even when they are trying to pronounce English.

This gives rise to what is called 'Japlish', a combination of English words with a Japanese pronunciation, a pronunciation that does not articulate these difficult and 'missing' sounds. When Japanese speakers speak Japlish foreign people accept this pronunciation as the best that the Japanese person can do. They do not want to correct the speaker and, consequently, the Japanese speakers of Japlish continue to make these mistakes but are under the illusion that they are, in fact, speaking Standard English.

While native English teachers quickly realize that there are no 'f', 'r' and 'v' sounds in Japanese, and initially do try to emphasize them, the regrettable truth is that they often give up trying to insist on correct pronunciation. Often they simply do not want to be disliked by their students. In any case, native English speakers are usually not going to stay in Japan for a long time and therefore rationalize that they will not be around to deal with the future difficulties that their students might get into!

(2) Do not be satisfied if other Asians understand you!
I recall one incident, when I was in my third year at London University. I was by this time quite familiar with different English accents and was able to place a speaker by listening to only a word or two. For instance, I could tell whether the speaker was from the southeast of England, or from the north. In particular, I was very fond of Scottish and Irish accents and indeed would often try to mimic them. One day, I was dining with a friend in a Chinese restaurant and I overheard one of the other diners speaking Japlish. I listened to the rhythm of his language and was quite convinced that he was Japanese.

During the meal, I took the opportunity to introduce myself to this person who certainly looked Japanese. It turned out that he was Korean, and I felt very lucky that I had addressed him in English and not Japanese, which he would not have understood: it could have been a rather embarrassing situation.

The point is, that, in my view, the rhythm of spoken Japanese is quite similar to the linguistic rhythm of Korean. Therefore, when either a Japanese or Korean speaker speaks English, the resulting rhythms are very similar. Japlish, therefore, is as understandable to another Japanese person as it is to most Koreans. Thus, the fact that your Japlish is under-stood by native Korean speakers of English is no indication that your English is being pronounced correctly.

(3) Remember, the English that you learn has to be understood worldwide!

English is undoubtedly the international language of our age. Why is this so? Before World War II, the British had colonized almost one third of the land surface of the world. While this extensive colonial empire began to disintegrate after the war, English remained the main language of education, commerce and administration in these former colonies, now 54 independent sovereign states. Additionally, the Americans – former colonialists of the British who achieved their independence in 1776 – became one of the great superpowers after the war. After the fall of the Soviet empire in the late 1980s, America became the only world super-power, with its language, culture and interests assuming great importance throughout the world.

In Japan, as in other countries, there are many who consider that English is what the Americans speak. However, there are differences between the vocabulary and the pronunciation of the English language as used by native English and American speakers. In this book, I will teach you Standard English, as spoken by the English. My aim is to teach you an English that is not simply understandable to good English speakers, but an English that is truly accepted and acceptable worldwide.

• Pronunciation (the sounds of English) first, then rhythm (accent, intonation, etc.) in learning English

(1) Do not learn languages solely from recorded tapes!

Almost a decade ago, Mr T. was still a student at Tokyo University. He was teaching mathematics part-time at my school and told me that he was interested in conversational English. One day, I mentioned to him that it would be all right if he were to sit in on an English class. He was excited at the opportunity and began learning conversational English.

His English (and it was American English), sounded very good to the Japanese in the class but it was really Japlish with a strong American English linguistic rhythm. I asked him where he had learned the language and he told me that he had learned it himself from a set of expensive American English recorded tapes.

As I have explained before, there are many English sounds that simply do not exist in Japanese. The Japanese cannot identify these sounds or produce them simply by listening to them and, so what they do is to conveniently change them into sounds that they can produce. Thus, the Japanese speaker thinks that he is pronouncing the numbers 733543 (seven, three, three, five, four, three) but actually what he/she is saying sounds more like 'seben, sulee, sulee, whibe, hor, sulee'. You can imagine the English person looking at him/her and saying 'Sorry?'. And as you can appreciate, whenever the Japanese speaker hears that 'Sorry?', he/she becomes confused and embarrassed, and begins to lose all confidence in his/her English-language skills.

Let me give you another personal anecdote regarding the problems involved with relying on recorded tapes to learn a language. After presenting my dissertation at London University, I decided to take a French course in France. A few years earlier, when I was at Oxford, I had taken private lessons with a French teacher and believed that my French language skills were at the intermediate level. I bought some tapes and worked on advancing my knowledge of the language. After about four months of working with these tapes, I felt that my French was so improved that I could now go to France.

Arriving at Charles de Gaulle Airport, outside Paris, I promptly tried out my French. Nobody understood me! I changed the intonation, the rhythm, the accent, but no matter what I did people simply did not understand the French that I spoke. I started to wonder whether my French teacher had been less than honest with me regarding my language skills. I was very disappointed and depressed. However, it occurred to me that French words are more difficult for the Japanese to pronounce than English ones, because there are sounds that are unique to French and not in either English or Japanese. To give an example, the French say that if a non-native speaker can pronounce 'rue' in French, then his/her pronunciation is good; a simple but effective test. While the idea might be simple, the work is still very difficult. For the next three months, thinking I would never be able to speak French in my entire life, I started learning French – particularly by isolating the unique French sounds and working hard on them – like I did in English. Surprisingly, however, much to my delight, after three months of assiduous work, I was able to speak and appreciate the language to a considerable degree.

My advice, then, is not to learn any language from recorded tapes alone. You must carefully identify the different sounds that occur in the foreign language but which are absent in Japanese, and concentrate on these. If you only rely on recorded tapes you will not be able to distinguish by listening to these sounds, consequently you will substitute sounds which can be pronounced by a Japanese person, and you will end up speaking Japlish, or its French equivalent.

(2) 'Light. I'll see you at sulee horty-whibe tomollow, Mr Bard', cannot be understood

I think that the rhythm of a language consists of its accent and intonation. If English were a song, the rhythm of the language would be the 'melody' of the language. And it is very important to acquire the rhythm of English in order to speak it well. But, before doing so, a Japanese person has to get himself/herself fully acquainted with the sounds of English which do not exist in Japanese.

Here is another example of the danger of learning English from recorded English tapes alone. Mr Aoki, with perfect English rhythm, might have intended to say: 'Right. I'll see you at three forty-five tomorrow, Mr Bird.' However, without those necessarily English sounds, much to Mr Bird's confusion, he would actually have said: 'Light. I'll see you at sulee horty-whibe tomollow, Mr Bard.' And, consequently, Mr Bird would have naturally reacted to this statement by saying, 'Sorry?'

On the other hand, having mastered those sounds of English which do not exist in Japanese, Mr Yamada with a monotonous Japanese linguistic rhythm might have said to Mr Bird: 'Right. I'll see you at three forty-five tomorrow, Mr Bird.' And Mr Bird would clearly understand Mr Yamada's statement. In other words, for a Japanese person the most important thing in learning English is to master those sounds of English which do not exist in Japanese.

You might understand this a little better if I use an example from Japanese. Suppose that a native Japanese speaker wants to say 'toli (bird)' but makes a slip of the tongue and says 'tali' instead. So, one Japanese person says to another Japanese speaker, 'Asokoni tali ga imasu ka?' ('Is there a bird over there?'), the listener would automatically say 'Sorry?', for the same reasons that Mr Bird would have said 'Sorry?' to Mr Aoki.

While 'right–light', and 'ban–van' sound more or less the same to the Japanese ear, the English listener hears them as quite distinct and different. That is to say, the differences between 'right' and 'light', and 'ban' and 'van' are greater in English than when a Japanese person mispronounces 'toli' for 'tali', because 'tali' has no meaning in Japanese, but in English 'right, light, ban' and 'van' have completely different meanings and are used frequently in everyday conversation.

Conversely, if an English person with a strong accent (that is like a rhythm) asks you in Japanese, 'Asoko ni tori ga imasu ka?' ('Is there a bird over there?'), it would not sound at all like natural Japanese because of the accent (or rhythm); however, you would very likely understand his/her sentence. Due to the fact 'tori' and 'toli' sound more or less the same to the Japanese ear, and because he/she pronounced all of the other sounds correctly, you would make sense of what he/she was saying. It is not difficult for this English speaker to say the sentence because most of the Japanese sounds are included in his/her own language. Indeed, today you will find that many foreign people speak Japanese on TV. However, in my view, foreign people who can speak Japanese with the correct linguistic rhythm, are few and far between.

In other words, the most important thing for Japanese students of English is to recognize the sounds of English which do not exist in Japanese. That is to say, the teaching of English to Japanese has to start from recognizing those sounds of English which are not in Japanese and to be able to correctly pronounce them.

Now we have a clearer understanding of the difficulties that native Japanese speakers should anticipate encountering in speaking English. These difficulties, however, can all be overcome: they are challenges waiting to be conquered. Remember, you will be able to speak English that is understood worldwide if you master those difficult sounds that are absent from the Japanese language. Now you are ready to start on the Kawata Method, so fully acquaint yourself with it by practising as much as possible – thereby allowing your conversational English to sound like a native English speaker.

Now you are ready to go on to the next chapter.

CHAPTER 2

☐ An introduction to the Kawata method

- ● The actual sound of 'R' as it is heard in words is formed like this – The Kawata R

IN THIS CHAPTER, I will outline the crucial aspects of the Kawata Method. Acknowledging the difference between English (vocal language) and Japanese (visual language), the Kawata Method advocates that in order to become proficient speakers of correct English the Japanese have to be able to pronounce the English sounds which do not exist in Japanese. *Inter alia*, 'the actual sound of R as it is heard in words', which native English speakers are not able to teach because they themselves are not taught how to pronounce it on its own at school, the Kawata Method shows clearly how the sound is formed with the Kawata R. Once you have become acquainted with the Kawata R your English will be intelligible to authentic English speakers and you will gain a mastery of conversational English.

(1) The two different 'R' sounds
In writing this book, I arranged interviews with many native speakers of English. Since they spoke naturally, they did not know where their tongue was when they pronounced the letter 'R' in words. Or rather, they simply took it for granted.

In my view, almost all the pronunciation problems of the Japanese are related to the fact that they cannot pronounce this sound 'R'. Despite the issue being talked about over and over again in Japan, namely that colloquial English is indispensable in the Japanese English Education System, and many native English speakers are involved in it, it remains a fact that the Japanese have a problem in becoming proficient at speaking correct English. Since native English teachers are unaware of how to pronounce 'the actual sound of R as it is heard in words' on its own, they are not able to teach it to the Japanese.

The most outstanding feature of the Kawata Method is to teach the learner 'the actual sound of R as it is heard in words' right from the beginning, together with the ordinary R(ɑ:) in the English alphabet.

Even young English children often get told off by their parents for not correctly pronouncing words which have the letter 'R' in them – for instance 'three, free, frog, etc.' in the correct way, because they are not taught in schools how to pronounce the actual sound of 'R' as it is heard in words. Their teachers and parents, who are quick to point out the error, find themselves unable to teach the correct method of pronunciation because they themselves were never taught how to prounounce it when they were young children.

The worst part of the English Conversational Education System in Japan is that the Japanese are so dependent upon native English teachers, and the Japanese never question the way they teach English. In fact, most of the native English-speaking teachers are unable to teach 'the actual sound of R as it is heard in words' to the Japanese, because they themselves have not been taught how to pronounce 'the actual sound of R as it is heard in words' on its own. I hope that in the near future this part of English education in England will be reviewed and that they will start teaching 'the actual sound of R as it is heard in words'.

(2) Master the alphabet correctly so as not to avoid mispronouncing 'sit' for 'shit'

If you have realized, 'English and Japanese are different! As English is a vocal language, a Japanese person has to start learning the sounds of English which are not in the language', you are heading in the right direction.

Then what does a Japanese person have to do in order to learn English? Firstly, you have to make yourself fully acquainted with the English alphabet and have to be able to pronounce each letter correctly. Among these sounds of the 26 letters of English there are some sounds which do not exist in Japanese. A Japanese person has to master those sounds. At the same time, those letters you might be wrongly pronouncing at the moment have to be relearned.

In the English alphabet, the sounds of letters which do not exist in Japanese are ' f, l, r, and v'. A Japanese person has to train his/her tongue and lips to pronounce the sounds of those letters well.

'A, C, J, K, O' are not properly pronounced in Japan. Consequently, the words which have those letters are wrongly transmitted and not understood by the English listener. For instance, 'C(si:)' is commonly pronounced '(ʃi:)' in Japanese. So when a Japanese person intends to say 'Sit down, please,' it becomes, 'Shit down, please'. An English person listening to it would be confused, as the actions of both expressions are similar to each other; if you do not know the meaning of the word 'shit', please look it up in your dictionary. And please make sure you can pronounce them correctly and distinctly.

'O(əu)', a diphthong, is another letter which is not properly pronounced in Japan. It is commonly pronounced as an elongated 'O(ɔ:)' sound. So a Japanese person tends to pronounce go(gɔ:), open(ɔ:pn). Also, I would like to draw your attention to the fact that only vowels are pronounced strongly in English. So take care not to pronounce them flatly with a Japanese rhythm.

(3) How the Kawata R (the actual sound of R as it is heard in words) is pronounced!

(a) Consonants are important in English, particularly 'f, l, r, v, θ' and 'ð' which do not exist in Japanese.

In learning English, the important sounds are the consonants. Particularly, it is very important for a Japanese person to be able to correctly pronounce consonants such as 'f, l, r, v, θ' and 'ð' which do not exist in Japanese. It is of vital importance to be aware that there are two 'Rs' in English, which sound totally different from one another, like chalk and cheese. How then can a Japanese person pronounce them? (cf. Illustration)

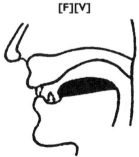

[F][V]

'Ff' and 'Vv'

The sounds of 'f' and 'v' are made by gently biting one's lower lip. In pronouncing 'f' a Japanese person tends to pronounce '(ehu)' with his mouth, but the correct sound of 'f' is made by gently biting the lower lip in the middle with the upper teeth while exhaling air, unvocalized. Similarly, the sound 'v' is made by gently biting the lower lip in the middle but this time, you vocalize the exhalation of air. The sound 'v' sounds like 'b' to the Japanese ear, but what one must not forget is that the sound 'v' in English is made only with one's lower lip.

'LI'

The sound 'LI' is created when one puts the tip of the tongue immediately behind the upper front teeth against the top gum. However, this sound is not that strict and has a certain variation of sounds. Actually, until the tongue reaches the point where the Kawata R is created the sounds of L are made possible.

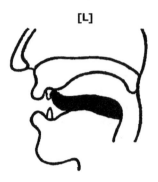

'Rr': There are two 'Rs' in English
The Ordinary 'R'

The sound of the ordinary 'R' in the English alphabet is created by keeping the tongue flatly resting on the bottom of the mouth behind the lower front teeth and make a sound R(ɑː) with the mouth slightly open.

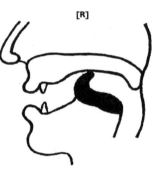

*
The Kawata R (the actual sound of 'R' as it is heard in words)

The Kawata R is created by the tongue. First pronounce 'L', then pull back the tongue from where you make the sound 'L' towards the throat 4–5cm along the palate (the ceiling of the mouth). If you roll the tip of the tongue slightly the sound will be stabilized. Make sure the tongue is touching the ceiling.

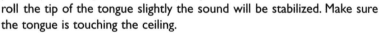

* This writer has to confess, however, that he is better at creating the actual sound of 'R' as it is heard in words this way rather than the traditional way of producing it – that is with both sides of the tongue touching the ceiling quite deep in the mouth towards the throat with the tip of the tongue not touching the ceiling. It is also his belief that his way of producing the actual sound of 'R' as it is heard in words should be easier, clearer and better-suited for the Japanese.

Here I would like to touch upon the sound of (ɜ:) which is similar to the sound of 'r'. For instance, 'return (ritɜ:rn)' has both (r) and (ɜ:). In this word there are two (r)s; in American English they are both pronounced, but in English only the first (r) is pronounced. This '(ɜ:)' is a peculiar English vowel, which one makes by half opening the mouth and pronouncing downwardly the sound found between an (ɑ) and (e). I must confess, for a Japanese person, this sound would be the most difficult sound to master in English.

(b) English will never become a real international lingua franca unless the other 'R' (the actual sound of R as it is heard in words) is taught in England.

The actual sound of R as it is heard in words is not presently being taught in schools in England. So the English people do not know how to pronounce the sound on its own, hence the reason why parents and teachers cannot teach it to their children and pupils.

In other languages there are similar sounds to the English 'R', for instance, they have (eɑ:r) in French, (Rru) in Spanish, (ɑh) in Arabic and so forth – therefore even though they are not pronouncing 'R' in the English way it is understood by the English as the sound 'R'.

In contrast, there is no such similar sound to the English 'R' (the actual sound of 'R' as it is heard in words) in Japanese. The closest sound is 'the Japanese L-like sound', which is also slightly different from the English 'L'.

It might not be a big problem in England as everyone over time is able to pronounce. But it is crucially important that a Japanese person is able to pronounce 'the actual sound of R as it is heard in words', or rather whether or not a Japanese person will be able to speak English greatly depends on it.

I would therefore suggest that English will never become a real international lingua franca unless 'the actual sound of R as it is heard in words' is taught and the non-native people, including Japanese, start speaking English with the proper English R, not with their Rs.

● The confusion caused by the Hepburn System

(1) 'Ra ri ru re ro' in the Hepburn System of Romanized script have to be changed immediately to 'la li lu le lo'

Whereas '*tori* (bird)' and '*toli*' almost sound the same to the Japanese ear, they sound completely different to English people. So for the Japanese 'ra ri ru re ro' as well as 'la li lu le lo' are the same as 'ラ (la) リ (li) ル (lu) レ (le) ロ (lo)' though, for the English they are clearly very different sounds.

A Japanese lady called 'Ritsuko' has recently started taking English conversation lessons at my school. She had a good reason to start, because she came to realize that she could not pronounce her own name as it is spelt in Japanese romanized script at the immigration section of an airport when she went abroad.

Looking into her passport the immigration officer said:

Officer: Your name is Ritsuko, isn't it?
Ritsuko: Yes, Litsuko.
Officer: No. Your name is Ritsuko, isn't it?
Ritsuko: Yes. My name is Litsuko.
Officer: No. Your name is Ritsuko, isn't it?
Ritsuko: Yes. My name is Litsuko.

This went on and on. But, she could not fathom what the problem was.

Within the Japanese education system, the sounds of 'ラ (la) リ (li) ル (lu) レ (le) ロ (lo)' are being taught to Romanize as 'ra ri ru re ro'. But the Japanese cannot pronounce 'ra ri ru re ro' as they do not have 'the actual sound R' (the Kawata R) in their language. I am advocating, therefore, that 'ra ri ru re ro' should be changed at once into 'la li lu le lo' which are almost the same as the Japanese pronunciation of 'ラ (la) リ (li) ル (lu) レ (le) ロ(lo)'. Unless this happens there will be more and more Japanese people who find themselves in the strange situation where they cannot pronounce their own names abroad. In order to avoid this, they should first of all change 'ra ri ru re ro' into 'la li lu le lo' and at the same time, by using the Kawata R, 'ra ri ru re ro' have to be also taught in contrast with 'la li lu le lo' when they teach children Romaji (the Romanized script of Japanese) at the elementary school.

In the case of 'ラ (la) リ (li) ル (lu) レ (le) ロ (lo)' in Japanese when I pronounce these letters, about 1 cm of the tip of the tongue is put flat behind the upper front teeth against the gum. The resulting sounds are slightly different from the English 'la li lu le lo' with only the tip of the

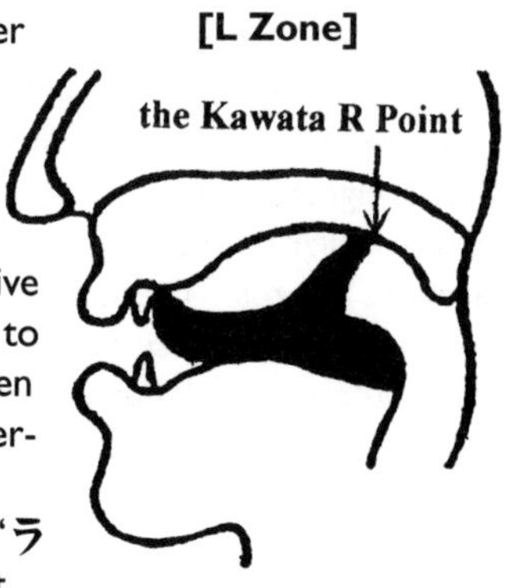

tongue pointedly put behind the upper front teeth against the top gum. However, as long as I have compared and studied those two different sets of sounds, 'ラ (la) リ (li) ル (lu) レ (le) ロ (lo)' and 'la li lu le lo', with native English and native American English teachers, I have come to the conclusion that the difference between them is very little and can be almost overlooked.

I have also found out that the sounds of 'ラ (la) リ (li) ル (lu) レ (le) ロ (lo)' are not that strict compared with 'la li lu le lo' using the English L and have a certain variation of sounds.

The Japanese sounds of 'ラ (la) リ (li) ル (lu) レ (le) ロ (lo)' can be achieved as long as the tip of the tongue stays in the L Zone (cf. Illustration), that is, until it reaches the Kawata R Point where 'the actual sound of R as it is heard in words' starts. Considering 'ra ri ru re ro' are presently used for 'ラ (la) リ (li) ル (lu) レ (le) ロ (lo)' in Japanese Romanized Script the difference could almost be ignored. In other words, the sounds of 'ラ (la) リ (li) ル (lu) レ (le) ロ (lo)' in Japanese are almost the same as 'la li lu le lo' with the English 'l' sound.

(2) Foreign people say they do not understand Japlish (Japanese English)!

I would now like to talk about Japanese loan words (*gailaigo*) taken mainly from English. In Japanese, most of the *gailaigo* are written in *katakana* (Japanese phonetic letters) in order to show that they have a foreign origin. But foreigners in Japan are confused by *katakana* loan words from English and other languages in Japanese. They think they are odd. As there are no sounds such as 'f, l, r, v, etc.' in Japanese, Japanese people pronounce '*bideo*' for 'video', '*camela*' for 'camera', '*lajio*' for 'radio' etc. They conveniently change the words into sounds they can pronounce and use them when speaking to foreigners.

Since the sounds of 'f, l, r, v, etc.' do not exist in their own language the Japanese people, from the outset, have imagined these things with changed pronunciations – changed in order to fit into their language, thus 'Japanized' pronunciations. On the reverse side of the coin, foreigners cannot imagine 'video' when they hear Japanese people saying '*bideo*'.

In recent years, increasing numbers of foreigners have been learning Japanese in this increasingly internationalized society in Japan, who along with the rest of the world are irritated by the fact that Japanese people cannot pronounce the sounds 'f, l, r, v,' etc.

There are many English phrases used in Japanese modern songs. When the foreigners listen to them, all they can think of is that, 'The words sound similar to English but they can't be English! They must be some new Japanese words.' Therefore, I would like you to get yourself fully acquainted with those English sounds which do not exist in Japanese so that you can confidently pronounce English.

I would like to introduce some Japanese song titles and pop-group names in both 'Japlish' and English.

First in 'Japlish':
Can you celeblate? Lide on time, All my tlue lobe, Ebely little sing, Kilolo.

This time in English:
Can you celebrate? Ride on time, All my true love, Every little thing, Kiroro.

It should now be clear why Japlish is not understood by non-Japanese.

So if Japanese people keep on using strange English in Japanese, without mastering those English sounds which do not exist in Japanese, the Japanese language itself will become a distorted, ridiculous and absurd language. And the world is really becoming tired of having to put up with those Japanese who keep on speaking strange English.

● Women are faster at learning languages. Be talkative. English is a catch-and-throw of sounds. Role-play being an English person. The more mistakes you make, the quicker you will learn English

It is said that women learn languages faster than men. I think this is because women are more receptive to sounds and more materialistic than men. Sound, once produced, becomes a material called a sound-wave and it is felt in their body. Women can sense the waves in the bodies more sensitively than men.

So it is no exaggeration to say that Japanese women should have an innate ability to speak English well. But if they do not make an effort their talent will be wasted. A diamond has to be polished to be a precious stone; otherwise it remains a worthless lump of glass.

If you are a 'talkative' person, please keep it up when you learn English. However, irrespective of gender, if you are composed, introverted, quiet and a typically traditional Japanese, in order to learn English I would like you to create another personality which is 'talkative and diplomatic' and role-play that person.

In the English-speaking world, there is no such thing as 'ishindenshin': reading each other's minds. Everything has to be expressed in sounds and conveyed to another person. You must play a catch-and-throw of sounds. So if you receive a sound, you have to give back a sound to the speaker. In doing so, 'Yes, Please, Thank you, Sorry, Ummmm, etc.' are very useful expressions when learning English. I would like you to use these expressions as often as possible and get yourself well accustomed to them.

Please discard your preconceptions of how to learn English, and try the Kawata Method. I would like you to role-play an English person even in an exaggerated manner. English is, for you English learners, a foreign language anyway. You can make as many mistakes as you like while learning it. The more mistakes you make the quicker you will learn the language.

All of this is an essential part of the Kawata Method, so please get used to it. You will actually quickly come to like it. You will also quickly come to speak excellent English. If you are ready we can now go on to some preparatory exercises.

CHAPTER 3

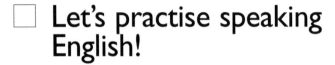 Let's practise speaking English!

Acquire the sounds of English which do not exist in Japanese.

NOW THAT YOU HAVE an idea of the key features of the Kawata Method you are ready to speak English.

The Kawata Method of learning conversational English is based on the thorough mastery of English pronunciation by the repeated practice of the sounds that cause particular difficulty for the Japanese speaker. In order to speak really good English, you must begin to build a solid foundation of clear and correct sounds.

Of course, there are always those students who want to move beyond this as quickly as possible and build up an impressive vocabulary. They end up with a lot of words that the native English speaker does not understand, not because they are unknown to the listener, but because the listener is unable to understand what the Japanese person is saying.

It is crucial that you start by getting yourself acquainted with the alphabet and are able to pronounce each letter clearly, distinctly and accurately. Only once this is done can we move on to the pronunciation of English words, with special attention to their vowels. To the Japanese learner, many English vowels may sound quite the same as one another, but they are not, and the Japanese speaker must be able to recognize the difference between them.

Before engaging in any kind of sports activity it is always sensible to do some kind of preparatory warm-up exercises; equally, before we begin to speak English we must do some 'warming-up' exercises. This is particularly true with those sounds that occur in English but not in Japanese: you must do preparatory exercises in order to practise getting your tongue, teeth and lips in the right place. You should go over these exercises until your tongue, teeth and lips begin to move naturally to form these sounds.

Vowels are stressed but consonants are to be clearly pronounced

The clear articulation of the alphabet is the key to good English-language skills. You must know the sound of the letters. Also, you must know that the English vowels are pronounced strongly. However, consonants have to also be clearly pronounced. For instance, the letters 'L', 'M', and 'N' when pronounced as letters of the alphabet all begin with the sound '(e)'. Thus, in producing the sound for the alphabet letter 'L', you begin with sound '(e)' and then form the rest of the sound with the tongue. With the 'M' and the 'N', you must clearly articulate the consonant. Thus, the consonants of 'M(emu)' and 'N(enu)', namely '[m'u']' and '[n'u']' have to be clearly and distinctly pronounced.

● Exercises In Pronunciation

In order to develop a better and more confident pronunciation, I would like you to do the following exercises. They are geared to helping you pronounce the sounds that are difficult for the Japanese speaker.

(1) Distinct pronunciation of the letters of the alphabet

Let us start by pronouncing the letters from A to Z. We know that some of these letters are difficult for the Japanese speaker, so concentrate on the ones that you have trouble with. The aim is to pronounce each letter distinctly and clearly, just as an English speaker would. Go through the alphabet, pronouncing each letter three times.

A (ei), B (biː), C (siː), D(diː), E (iː), F(ef)
G (dʒiː), H (eitʃ), I (ɑi), J (dʒei), K (kei),
L (el), M (em), N (en), O (əʊ), P (piː), Q (kjuː)
R (ɑː), S (es), T (tiː), U (juː), V (viː), W (dʌbliju),
X (eks), Y (wai), Z (English 'zed' or American 'ziː')

Now try pairing letters that sound similar to the Japanese ear. You should make sure that each of the letters is sounded clearly. This is not easy; however, part of the Kawata Method is training your tongue and lips. At first this will not seem natural for you: you have to learn how it is to be done. Once you have accustomed your tongue and lips to producing these sounds they become part of your way of speaking and your pronounced English will be clear and distinct.

BV,	BV,	BV
FS,	FS,	FS
LR,	LR,	LR
MN,	MN,	MN

(2) Pronunciation of words with English sounds that do not exist in Japanese

These are difficult words that the Japanese often get wrong. But you are going to get it right! Pronounce each of these words slowly and correctly. At first you may well have difficulty with the sounds because they do not exist in Japanese. Do not rush through the exercise. Make every one of these difficult letters clear and deliberate. With the (w), Japanese people often mix this sound up with the Japanese ウ <u> sound. It is particularly difficult to make after a consonant. You should make a very conscious effort to push out the lower lip when you make this sound.

(f)   fine, fish, foot, fast, fight, finish
(l)   London, lion, letter, little, lily, lock, look
(r)   Rome, room, rain, road, ring, rock, red
(v)   village, volleyball, vacation, vegetable, violin
(w) twin, twig, twenty, twelve, swim, sweet, sweat, swing, Sweden

(3) Pronouncing letters that are usually pronounced incorrectly in Japan

Here are a group of sounds that are often mispronounced by the Japanese. Let us look at each in turn and try to understand what the sound is like and why you might have difficulty in pronouncing it correctly. Once you can appreciate the difficulties, your English pronunciation will become like that of a Standard English speaker.

‘A’ must be pronounced ‘(ei)’ and never ‘an elongated sound (e:)’. Try to get this with:

table, day, change, exchange, strange, arrange, pray

'O' is pronounced '(əʊ)' and should never be pronounced '(ɔ:)'.

low, go, no, open, bold, gold, told, row, road, load

In contrast, some words really do possess the '(ɔ:)' and you should try to distinguish between this next set of words and the last one:

ball, fall, call, all, hall, bought, fought, bald, saw, raw, wall

'C' is pronounced '(si:)'; remember the problems that you can get your-self into if you pronounce this as '(ʃi:)'. Differentiate between the following set of sounds:

(si<:>)   sip, see, sit, seep, sell, single
(ʃi<:>)   ship, she, shit, sheep, shell, shingle

(4) Pronouncing letters that are often confused

Here, you will make a conscious effort to clarify the pronunciation of letters that the Japanese often confuse. The first difficult pair is (b) and (v); the second is (l) and (r). Try to be careful in getting these letters correct:

(b)   best, boat, bow, bent, bet, bat, berry
(v)   vest, vote, vow, vent, vet, vat, very
(l)   low, law, lice, fly, light, long, life, lend
(r)   row, raw, rice, fry, right, wrong, rife, rend

(5) Pronouncing words with two or more sounds not existing in Japanese

Again, you must make sure that you pronounce each letter distinctly. Do not try to rush through the word, slow down and deal with each syllable. Try these combination words:

(l) and (r)   really, generally, already, library, traditionally, realise, probably
(f) and (l)   flour, flower, family, full, fool, fold, follow, fellow, floor
(r) and (v)   several, drive, very, varied, various, travel, brave
(f) and (v)   fever, five, forgive, festival, favourable, forever
(f) and (r)   fruit, friend, from, froth, freedom, traffic, roof

(6) Pronouncing (ɑ<:>), (ʌ), (æ) and (ɜ:)

This group of four sounds, (ɑ<:>), (ʌ), (æ) and (ɜ:), also presents difficul-ties for the Japanese speaker. All of these sounds are similar to, but not the same as, the Japanese sound ' ア (ɑ)'. Of these four sounds, the first '(ɑ<:>)' is very close to the Japanese sound however, the other three are not the same and do not exist in Japanese. Let us practise these difficult sounds. You should practise them until you are able to produce them well. This will take some time but you will succeed so long as you have a clear understanding of what the sound is supposed to be.

Let us practise these.

As we said this sound is very like the Japanese ' ア (ɑ)':
(ɑ<:>) glass, grass, fast, dark, dart, heart, cart, barter

This sound is more like a short exclamation of surprise as in words like:
(ʌ) cut, cup, bun, fun, run, touch, done, none, gun, sun, nut

A slightly compressed version of (ɑ) that somewhere between (ɑ) and (e): (æ) apple, ant, jam, accident, fact, cat, rat, sat, mat, fat, van, fan

This is a sound that is peculiar to the English language. It is made by half opening the mouth and pronouncing a sound downwards somewhere between (ɑ) and (e). Here are some examples of this sound:

(ɜ:) first, early, girl, her, dirty, thirty, nurse, bird, circle, purple, curtain

(7) Pronouncing the two different 'th' sounds
As you will recall, in English there are two different ways of pronouncing 'th'. In one (θ), the sound is made by putting the tip of the tongue between the upper and lower teeth and then exhaling. However in the other (ð), the sound is produced in the same way but this time the sound is vocalized. Naturally, since both of these sounds are written in the same way, you have to learn which is which. In this exercise take care to distinguish between the two different sounds.

(θ) three, third, throat, throw, Thursday, threat, think, thin
(ð) they, these, those, with, breathe

(8) Pronouncing letter combinations that do not exist in Japanese
In the exercise that follows, pay special attention to the sound combinations that we do not have in the Japanese language. You should make sure that you pronounce each individual sound.

'r' drink, green, ready, recipe, interest, rush, strong, origin, dictionary, century, Europe, bread, abroad, brought, around, trade, rich, Korea,

cross, operation, dream, agree, produce, report, precious, ground, rise, recovery, treatment, praise, price, brave, bright, raise, truth
'v' invite, drive, village, drove, given, however, various, themselves, heavy, everywhere, receive, servant, service, valley, very
'f' beef, before, freedom, festival, from, free, knife, traffic, forgiven, fruit, photograph, friend, family, fellow, fun, flames, phrase, foreigner

(9) Pronouncing words that contain Japanese vowel sounds

These words all have vowel sounds in them that you are familiar with in Japanese. Go over the list pronouncing everything, as usual, three times. Focus on the accurate and clear pronunciation of each word. You should know these words, but if you do not, make sure that you find out what they mean from your dictionary. We indicate the vowel sound for each of the sets of words:

(i)	big, film, pig, fish, fit, hit, sit, bit
(i:)	bee, beach, sea, see, cookie, green, beaver, receive, eager, fever
(u)	foot, look, good, cook, wood, should, hood
(u:)	room, lose, school, food, fool, root, loot
(e)	egg, hen, red, elephant, edge, let, men, shell, wet, lend
(ɔ)	clock, hot, lock, rock, cod, rob, conscious, contradict
(ɔ:)	ball, fall, call, hall, all, tall, bought, ought
(ai)	high, buy, pie, lie, right, pipe, sight, die, fight, site, kite
(au)	loud, sound, ground, how, row, bow,
(ɔi)	joy, toy, boy, oil, noisy, choice, join, moisture, soil

(10) General pronunciation exercise

The words introduced here have either English sounds, which do not exist in Japanese, or are words that sound more or less the same to Japanese people, yet are pronounced differently in English.

(1) Practise pronouncing the words so as to be able to clearly distinguish them.

(2) Practise listening to them so as to be able to distinguish the words.

Note: Words which may have more than one pronunciation have Standard English phonetic signs after them.

START
1. low 2. row (rəu)
3. berry 4. belly 5. very
6. best 7. vest 8. bow (bau) 9. vow
10. light 11. right 12. rice 13. lice
14. ban 15. bun 16. van 17. fan 18. fun
19. glass (glɑːs) 20. grass (grɑːs) 21.lock(lɔk) 22.rock(rɔk)
23. loom 24. room 25. bet 26. vet 27. ran 28. run
29. load 30. road 31.see 32. she 33. raw 34. law
35. rub 36. love 37. bust 38. vast 39. fry 40. fly
41. play 42. pray 43. work 44. walk 45. rat 46. rut
47. rent 48. lent 49. bank 50. bunk 51. hat 52. hut

(11) Pronouncing complete sentences

Words by themselves, of course, do not constitute conversational English. While it is crucial that you are able to pronounce letters and words clearly and correctly, you have to be able to do that in the context of conversation.

In order to help you with this I have devised the following exercise, which is in three parts. In the first, you will read and correctly pronounce a list of words, whose initial letters follow the alphabet. In the second and third parts of the exercise, you will use these words in a conversational setting. You should work on this exercise with one or two fellow students. Take turns asking the questions that I have set and listen to one another.

Facility and confidence in conversational English come about by hard work and repeated practice. You have to speak but you have to listen as well. In future, when you speak English, nobody will give you a script to read and nobody will write down his or her answer. It is essential that at the very beginning you develop the ability to listen carefully and respond accurately. You will make mistakes at the beginning and that is all right; making mistakes will let you find out what is difficult for you. Once you realize your mistakes you can go about correcting them. Now, proceed with the exercise.

(1) First read these words:

agree, bury, century, dictionary, everywhere, festival, grand, history, igloo, judgment, kingdom, load, mustard, nurse, original, precious, queen, recovery, Switzerland, twelfth, urgent, various, waterproof, xylophone, yawn, zoology

(2) Use these words

Use them in the following conversational structure. Remember to clearly articulate all of the words that you use.

A: What word comes before 'recovery', please?
B: 'Queen.' 'Queen' comes before 'recovery'.
A: How do you spell it, please?
B: It's spelt 'Q-U-E-E-N.'
A: Would you pronounce it again, please?
B: Yes. 'Queen.'
A: Thank you. ↓
B: Thank you. ↑

Continue using this above structure, with the next student selecting a different word.

(3) A further conversational approach

Here is another conversational setting to give you confidence with using these words. Again, while these sentences are very short and direct they will help you practise the sounds and combinations of sounds that we have learned so far.

A: Would you tell me the word starting with the letter 'N,' please?
B: Yes. 'Nurse.'
A: How many letters are there in the word?
B: There are 'five (letters).'
A: What are they?
B: They are 'N-U-R-S-E.'
A: Thank you.
B: Not at all.

CHAPTER 4

Primary school English education

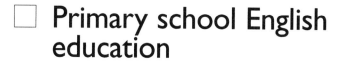

Can English be taught without a native English instructor?

LET US LOOK for a moment at the history of teaching English in our primary schools. A few years ago there had been a great deal of discussion going on across the country regarding the usefulness of teaching English to our primary school students. Finally, in 2002, they started teaching English in primary schools. Since then, various problems have been identified.

One of the major problems is that Japanese teachers cannot communicate in English with native English teachers. Consequently, the cooperation between the native English teachers and the Japanese primary school teachers seems to be rather difficult to achieve. However, as it has been advocated in Chapter 2 that many native English teachers are unable to teach the actual R sound as it is heard in words to the Japanese, which is an indispensable sound for the Japanese to acquire in order to speak English correctly, they should not be too dependent on native English teachers to teach them English anyway.

Whereupon I devised a method whereby primary school teachers themselves can teach English to their students without resorting to a limited number of native English teachers and native English speakers in Japan. By using the Kawata Method, primary school teachers will be able to teach conversational English that is clear, well articulated and readily understood anywhere in the world. So, if you are a primary school teacher, you should appreciate that the skills and clarity in pronunciation that you learn in the Kawata Method will help you teach your students without even requiring native English-speaking instructors.

Many teachers feel awkward about this. They believe that the reason we have native English speakers teaching English is because the Japanese person is not really capable of teaching English. This is erroneous. However, you do need to be carefully trained before the clarity of your pronunciation will be adequate. The way in which our children can acquire good English-language skills is not by employing more native English speakers. Rather, it is by primary school teachers taking up the challenge and by practising, practising and practising their English pronunciation.

● Practise and practise again!

There is a secret in the Kawata Method, a secret that you have undoubtedly discovered already. While we would all like to rush into English conversation as soon as possible, the Kawata Method recognizes that you cannot produce good quality, understandable English until you have a command and mastery of the sounds of the language. There is no way of taking a short-cut because these sounds are the essential way in which meaning is conveyed. If you have not mastered these English sounds you will not be understood.

That is why I make no apology for asking you to repeat the exercises that were introduced in the first part of this chapter. Careful articulation, careful listening and constant practice are the keys to success. However, this time as we go through these essential exercises, I will introduce ideas and suggestions about how you can use these in the classroom setting and how you can encourage your students to make good progress in acquiring these essential language skills. So, while we looked at things from the student's perspective earlier on, here I want you to consider your role as a teacher.

Before beginning, let me make a few comments on ways that you can create a positive environment for teaching English. Firstly, you should try to conduct as much of your lesson in English as possible. This will not be easy but a few simple ideas will help you to do this. Remember that your students will gain enormously by being exposed to the English language and by having that language repeated. Start by introducing simple but commonly-used English expressions. Use these as the basis for exercises. Repeat them, and repeat them in different forms. Introduce variety into your lesson but do not confuse repetition with being monotonous.

• Some simple but powerful words:

'*Sorry?*' ↑ When English people want you to repeat something they do not say so directly. So instead of actually saying, 'Could you repeat that, please?' they simply say, 'Sorry?' But the word is only half of the story. I have marked it with the sign (↑), indicating that the intonation rises. The upturning intonation often signals a question, as in this case. When you hear that slightly upturning intonation you know that either the other person has not heard what you said, or has heard it but does not understand. Do you think that you understand this? 'Sorry?' ↑

'Sorry!' ↓ The same word, but here the intonation drops down. This is not a question being asked but rather an apology being given. So, when you are in a restaurant and somebody bumps into you and spills your coffee, he says, 'Sorry!' ↓

'Thank you.' ↑ Here, with a rising intonation, the speaker stresses the word 'you'. You will generally hear the English using this when someone has thanked them. They could also have used phrases like, 'Not at all, it's my pleasure', or 'Please don't mention it'. So when someone thanks you for having helped him, or her, in some way it is a polite and well-mannered thing to simply say, 'Thank you.' ↑

'Thank you.' ↓ In this case you wish to thank somebody. A slight stress goes on the 'thank', and the intonation falls slightly. These are very little words but they are very powerful. Could you please practise the rising and falling intonations of these? *Thank you.* ↓

'Please.' When you ask someone to do something for you, you use this expression.

'Yes.' Nodding is not enough, one has to utter a sound.

'Ummmm ....' Pronounced 'ʌmmmmm..... ', this is used in English when one is thinking, or gets stuck in a conversation.

Now that we have learned the simple but powerful words, I urge you to use them with your students. They will help considerably with the flow of words and conversation. Use them whenever you can. They also train your students to listen for the ways in which intonation rises or falls, creating a different meaning.

Now let us resume practising.

(1) Distinct pronunciation of the letters of the alphabet

Remember that pronunciation is the vital foundation on which you will build your students' language skills. If they cannot pronounce these letters they will not be able to speak intelligible English. Build the foundation stone. Repeat, correct, repeat, correct . . . Require your students to listen and to actually hear what sounds come out of their mouths. So begin by carefully going through the alphabet making sure that these letters are understood and articulated well. Right from the beginning, things should be repeated aloud three times.

A (ei),   B (bi:),   C (si:),   D(di:),   E (i:),   F (ef)
G (dʒi:),   H (eitʃ),   I (ɑi),   J (dʒei),   K (kei),
L (el),   M (em),   N (en),   O (əʊ),   P (pi:),   Q (kju:)
R (ɑ:),   S (es),   T (ti:),   U (ju:),   V (vi:),   W (dʌblju),
X (eks),   Y (wai),   Z (English 'zed' or American 'zi:')

Once the letters are mastered you can begin to pair the sounds. Here, I have put them together in ways that are difficult for the Japanese speaker. The Kawata Method is all about training the tongue and lips. Be prepared to demonstrate this with your students. Be confident, practise, be skilled at carefully and clearly sounding each letter in the pair. Again, say these three times aloud. Just as when you exercise, you need to physically warm up, so too in speaking English: the tongue, teeth and lips must be warmed up.

BV,   BV,   BV
FS,   FS,   FS
LR,   LR,   LR
MN,   MN,   MN

(2) Listening and writing exercises for the alphabet

Your students must listen carefully. They will want to learn the proper order of the letters in the alphabet, which is very important. However, they must also be able to identify (by sound) single letters and write these down. Have your students listen to you read letters of the alphabet randomly. For instance you could say something like this:

Qq, Ww, Ee, Rr, Tt, Yy, Uu, Ii, Oo, Pp, Ll, Kk, Jj, Hh, Gg, Ff, Dd, Ss, Aa, Zz, Xx, Cc, Vv, Bb, Nn, Mm.

(3) Identifying letters from the alphabet

You can also get your students to appreciate the sequence of letters by playing the following game. Note, that while you are teaching the letters of the alphabet you are also engaging the students in conversation. Get them used to speaking. Get them used to speaking clearly with every word carefully pronounced. Ask them to repeat words if you do not hear them, or if they are poorly formed. Instill in your students the idea that learning English is not difficult but that it does require care, patience and constant repetition of clear, well-produced sound.

Try this more conversational format:

A: Which letter comes before 'Ff,' please?
B: 'Ee.' 'Ee' comes before 'Ff .'
A: Which letter comes after 'Ff,' please?
B: 'Gg.' 'Gg' comes after 'Ff.'
A: Thank you. ↓
B: Thank you. ↑

(4) Use of numbers – from one to ten

Begin by making sure that the students can pronounce the first ten numbers clearly and correctly. You should pay particular attention to the numbers 'three', 'four', 'five' and 'seven'. All of these normally present difficulties for Japanese speakers. Ask your students to count:

one, two, three, four, five, six, seven, eight, nine, ten

Once the individual numbers have been articulated clearly, you can try a more conversational style, one which asks the student to correctly pronounce the number within a sentence. This is going to be a little more difficult for some students. Try this exercise:

A: What number comes before 'three', please?
B: Two.' 'Two'comes before 'three'.
A: What number comes after 'three', please?
B: Four. 'Four' comes after 'three'.
A: Thank you. ↓
B: Thank you. ↑

(5) Now, let's get more conversational!

For this exercise, have each of the students stand in front of the class and role-play person 'A' in the script given below. The remaining class members will play the part of 'B' – in chorus, all speaking together. We encourage the class to use the English 'Sorry?' and to ask the student to repeat the words or phrase when his or her English is not clear enough or loud enough. All of the students should be encouraged to enter into this exercise. This preparation will be of considerable help when they have to engage in conversation. Teach the class to listen and speak. Teach them to be direct and responsive.

A: Hello.
B: Hello.
A: I'll ask you some questions. Please answer my questions.
B: Yes.
A: Which letter comes before 'Rr', please?
B: 'Qq.' 'Qq' comes before 'Rr'.
A: Which letter comes after 'Rr', please?
B: 'Ss.' 'Ss' comes after 'Rr'.
A: What number comes before 'five', please?
B: 'Four.' 'Four' comes before 'five'.
A: What number comes after 'five', please?
B: 'Six.' 'Six' comes after 'five'.
A: Thank you.
B: Not at all.

(6) Pronunciation with sentences

There are three exercises in this section. In the first we will deal with words, then with sentences. In the first exercise, be careful to pronounce these vowels and consonants properly.

apple, boat, cat, dog, egg, fish, good, house, ice, jam, king, lion, milk, name, orange, pig, queen, room, ship, table, umbrella, village, water, xylophone, yacht, zoo.

Now, try using the words in the above alphabetic list in the following structure. Again, while the word by itself might be pronounced correctly you must make sure that it is still pronounced clearly and correctly within the sentence.

A: What word comes before 'fish', please?
B: 'Egg.' 'Egg' comes before 'fish'.
A: How do you spell it, please?
B: It's spelt 'E-G-G'.

A: Would you pronounce it again, please?
B: Yes. 'Egg'.
A: Thank you. ↓
B: Thank you. ↑

Finally, use the words in the alphabetical list in this more expanded sentence structure.

A: Would you tell me the word starting with the letter A, please?
B: Yes. 'Apple'.
A: How many letters are there in the word?
B: There are five (letters).
A: What are they?
B: They are 'A-P-P-L-E'.
A: Thank you.
B: Not at all.

Move round the class asking students to make up these questions using all of the words in the initial list. In this exercise, the central feature is to encourage all of the students to articulate the words clearly and to hear them being pronounced. If a student makes a mistake, encourage the rest of the class to correct this. These exercises are participatory, with all class members taking part.

CHAPTER 5

Because you are Japanese, you have got to be able to speak English well!

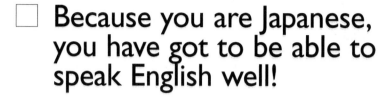

The Japanese have an innate ability to speak English well, so now get the rhythm of English right.

IT MAY SOUND STRANGE, but one of the difficulties with the Kawata Method is that your English pronunciation might actually become too good! To illustrate what I mean by this, let me provide a few examples that have involved some of my former students. Perhaps from their experience you will begin to see what can happen when you learn to speak English using the Kawata Method.

● Four success stories

(1) Surprises in South Africa

About twenty years ago, when I returned to Japan from my studies in France, I started to teach English and French. One day, a medical doctor, whom I knew, approached me and asked if I would give him a crash course in conversational English. He had to visit South Africa on a professional matter for about five weeks and it was essential that he could speak a high level of English. His professional English skill level was high but conversational skill level was not that fluent. We began a one-month crash course.

In South Africa, two European languages are spoken: Afrikaans (which is a variant of Dutch), and English. This language diversity reflects the history of the country, which was initially settled by both farmers from Holland (the Boers) and by the English. South Africa is a former British colony and English is readily understood throughout the country, being used as the main language of commerce. Although the English spoken in South Africa has a very distinctive accent, I knew that if my friend had a sound basis of clearly articulated British English, he would be understood in the country.

After the crash course, my medical friend went to South Africa. Five weeks later, on his return to Japan, he telephoned me with the following message: 'Mr Kawata, I must tell you that the English you taught me got me into a lot of trouble! The problem was that when people heard me speak they were convinced that my level of English language comprehension was much higher than it really was! I can honestly tell you that my English pronunciation turned out to be simply too good!'

It was very amusing, but there was a serious side to what this former student told me. When he spoke the language, he articulated so clearly that people hearing him thought he was a very accomplished English speaker. What was very gratifying for me was, that in that one-month crash course, I had been able to correct his pronunciation to such a degree that people not only understood what he was saying but were convinced that he was an excellent English speaker. In any event, even though he was often engaged in conversation that he could not fully appreciate, he told me that the five-week tour of duty had gone exceptionally well. He thanked me for what I had been able to accomplish, and I have no doubt that his excellent performance on the tour was in part the result of the confidence and the credibility that the Kawata Method gave him.

(2) Surprises in Australia

A second story that comes to mind took place some ten years ago, when one of my school's part-time maths teachers decided to go to Australia with his friend. While this young man confided in me that his English was poor, he was very pleased that his friend had earned an English Language Proficiency Certificate in Japan. He thought that together, they would have no problems with the language. However, just to be on the safe side, he decided that he would take some English pronunciation classes at my school. There were only four weeks left until they were due to depart for Australia, but he attended the classes and worked very hard on essential English sounds which do not exist in Japanese.

On his return to Japan, this young man came to visit me. He had been flabbergasted! It turned out that when he and his friend were in Australia, people could not understand his friend's pronunciation. While undoubtedly his friend had a much better vocabulary and command of the English language, it did not help: he was constantly misunderstood. On the other hand, this young man was clearly understood and even his basic English skills could be used to the maximum.

In both the South African and Australian cases, the people involved had hardly any prior experience of conversational English before they joined my classes. In the month that we had to work with these people, we were not able to give them a comprehensive vocabulary. However, every word that they had they could use. The reason? The Kawata Method concentrates on accurate and clear articulation. Literally every word that they had pronounced was clearly understood. However, with the person who possessed an English Language Proficiency Certificate, even a rich vocabulary and an extensive knowledge of idiomatic conversational English got him nowhere as English speakers were not able to understand what he was saying.

(3) The experiences of an ex-stewardess

The Kawata Method works! Mrs M.K., an ex-stewardess, who has got herself thoroughly acquainted with the Kawata Method, tells the following story of her experiences in her own words.

It really worked wonders! Soon after learning English with Mr Kawata, many foreign passengers praised me for the announcements that I made on board the plane. Up until then, because of my profession I had tried various methods of learning English such as using expensive audio tapes and thick English textbooks but they all turned out to be completely useless. Only knowing English words and phrases wasn't enough.

Having come through all the other methods, I have encountered a really effective method of learning English at last. This is what I call a real method of learning English conversation. It has become much more fun to speak English as every word I utter is understood!

Through thoroughly exercising the basic sounds of English and the sounds of English which do not exist in Japanese, the Kawata Method has drastically changed my English. I know that many acquaintances of mine have had the same kind of experiences as I have.

If you wish to learn English conversation, try the Kawata Method first, I strongly recommend it. After taking off with the Kawata Method, you can use any textbook of English or recorded tapes. I, therefore, confidently say that it is absolutely a must to start learning English with the Kawata Method.

I was delighted with Mrs M.K.'s success. As a stewardess she had to be excellent in her communication using English. Again, it has been very gratifying to hear that this method is effective, and I thank Mrs M.K. for her testimonial.

(4) Mr M.O. from a multi-national company

For the fourth story of the success of the Kawata Method, I would like to tell you about Mr M.O. who was to present his research in English before a large array of learned scientists in the United States of America. He did not know how he was going to do this and was quite concerned about the prospect of having to perform the presentation in English. I had only six months to work with him, however, during that time, I was able to introduce him to English sounds and in particular those tricky sounds that appear in English but not in Japanese. After the presentation this is what Mr M.O. wrote:

> In order to prepare for my research presentation in the United States of America, I studied with Mr Kawata for six months. During that period I concentrated on the pronunciation of English. I must say that at the beginning my English skills were very poor and I did not even like to speak the language. However, at the end of the six months not only was my English pronunciation improved but also I was confident in speaking the language; in fact, I really learned the joys of using English.
>
> After my presentation, several people in the audience called out, 'Nice presentation!' This was very gratifying and rewarding for me. I am very pleased to have studied with Mr Kawata. My improved ability in speaking English has given me tremendous faith in the Kawata Method. I can recommend it without reservation, and I would like those of you who read this to experience the same excitement as I did.

Again, I was very pleased with the progress that Mr M.O. made in our private lessons. However, the essential thing is that his hard work was able to bring maximum results. The Kawata Method is designed to allow you to speak in a manner that is understood by others. In Mr M.O.'s case, he was able to communicate very effectively with very sophisticated users of the English language. I was delighted with his oratorical success and equally pleased that this success was in part attributable to the use of the Kawata Method.

● The Kawata Method shall rescue Japan from the recession

As the above stories indicate, speaking intelligible English results in a great many personal advantages and rewards. However, it is not simply personal advantages that are to be gained from the ability to speak English – there are national and economic benefits as well.

(1) The competitive edge

Japan is still in the most serious economic recession since World War II. Although there are many stated factors that have contributed to this economic downturn, in my view, there are only a few real causes, and the main one, which I feel has been given too little consideration, is the way in which we in Japan learn and speak English.

For many years there has been general agreement that English is the primary language in international business. It is an advantage for business people to be able to speak good English. Also, for a nation, training people to speak English competently gives that country a competitive edge – certainly in business, and also in science and cultural activities.

Regrettably, Japan has earned a reputation as a place that is not 'English friendly'; furthermore, the language is not widely used and it is taught poorly. This has resulted in many multinational corporations relocating their corporate headquarters from Japan to countries like Singapore, which has a better record of working with English.

In order to make a positive impact on the economic recession that Japan is suffering from, we should change our image. Instead of being seen as a country that is bad at English, we have to become recognized as a place where our citizens excel in the learning and speaking of that language. This would restore a vital and a significant competitive edge that has been lost. In order for this to come about the whole system of teaching English within the Japanese educational system must be revised. At present, the language is being taught poorly with students unable to use what they are taught. They are hindered by their poor pronunciation: it is simply too difficult for English speaking people to try to understand what they are saying.

We must change the emphasis in English teaching in Japan. We must focus on allowing our students to acquire a practical, understandable, conversational English that they can use effectively. While the Japanese educational authorities have decided that English should now be taught in the primary school system, there is still a lack of clarity about what kind of English will be taught, who will teach it, and what the emphasis of the language classes will be. With the Kawata Method, I am advocating that irrespective of one's age, one is able to master conversational English, though it is always good to learn a foreign language when one is young, and so I applaud the decision to start teaching our children younger. But this advantage could easily be lost unless we clarify our goals. From my experience, it is essential that we start by producing young people who can articulate English in a meaningful way. Then they would enjoy speaking English, and would help to correct the negative image that so many people have formed about the Japanese and their relationship with the English language.

(2) The efficiency of learning British (or Standard) English

Today, the United States, as everyone knows, is the biggest ecomomic power in the world. Since the end of World War II, the United States of America and Japan have enjoyed good and stable relations. These strong ties exist in commercial and cultural spheres. Given this affinity, it is only natural that many Japanese people firmly believe that English is what the Americans speak!

I am afraid that this is not so. There are many forms of spoken English, and the American variety is one of them – albeit a very popular and widely used form. My point is that we do not have to give up our close connections with the Americans by speaking non-American English. In fact, those ties will become stronger when our American friends and associates hear why we have to use somewhat easier British (or Standard) English.

What I mean is this. Although I advocate that the Japanese have to make themselves acquainted with Standard English first, I am not against the idea of accepting regional accents in Britain or different versions of English spoken in various countries. What I am trying to say is that for the Japanese, whose language is uniquely visual in which some essential sounds of English are missing, Standard English is the most suitable version of English because of the way it is articulated and intelligibly pronounced, thus making it both clearer to comprehend and oratorically less challenging for the Japanese.

The Japanese find it very hard to speak American English because: (a) it contains more 'R' sounds, and (b) it has significantly greater incidences of nasal sounds than in Standard (British) English. That is another reason why the Kawata Method is so successful: it centres on good Standard English and teaches this carefully. While this method uses British English as its model, it does not necessarily mean that those who teach it must themselves be native (British) speakers – quite the contrary. If you speak Japanese yourself, even if you speak it very well and are considered very accomplished in that language, you might discover that you are not such a good teacher of Japanese. In a very real sense you know the language too well – you know it from the perspective of a Japanese person, not from the point of view of a foreigner. But it is the non-Japanese who have to learn Japanese!

The Kawata Method of learning conversational English is a way of teaching 'Standard English' without worrying too much about the limited number of native English speakers in Japan. If you have ever taught Japanese to foreigners, you would know being able to speak Japanese well is one thing but being able to teach Japanese well is another. One learns to speak one's own language naturally and instinctively. So being able to speak English well is not the same as being able to teach it well. When one teaches a Japanese person English, the most important thing is to clearly indicate those sounds of English that do not exist in Japanese and to teach the student how to pronounce them. Regrettably, it seems that most of the native English speakers are not good at teaching English since their ability to speak English was acquired naturally and instinctively.

By all means, the Kawata Method focuses on these very difficulties. The Kawata Method is specifically designed for the Japanese speaker to learn conversational English. I have made an extensive study of the English language and because I am a native Japanese speaker myself, I appreciate the problems and challenges that the Japanese student will face when learning English. The method that I have devised will allow those learning and teaching English to concentrate on the problems and to overcome them. I deliberately direct my students to the problem areas in English pronunciation because I am aware that these difficulties inevitably occur with native Japanese speakers. Learning English by the Kawata Method will ensure that you speak English in a manner that is internationally recognized. The Americans will not only understand your Standard English pronunciation, they are actually fond of good Standard English compared to badly spoken American English.

• The Japanese have an innate ability to speak English well!

If you have followed the arguments in this chapter, you might conclude that if you practise the difficult English sounds and acquire the English vocabulary presented in Japanese Compulsory Education (that is, up to the age of fifteen), you would be able to speak English well. However, I would like to explain the difference between simply speaking English and speaking the language well.

(1) I didn't understand, 'Are you from Tokyo?'

Recently, I was having a conversation with two English people when I became aware that they were constantly making use of a word that I did not understand. Although I knew it might have been somewhat impolite, I stopped them and asked what this word was. The word turned out to be the Japanese word 'noh(能)'. When it was used with an English pronunciation and rhythm it had seemed to me to be a very strange and unfamiliar word indeed. Incidentally, the reason that they were discussing 'noh' was that one of their friends was writing a master's dissertation on the subject at Tokyo University. So although I knew the word, the pronunciation and the rhythm of the speech totally confused me.

Here is another example to underscore the point, this time taken from my experience in England. I was a postgraduate student at London University and felt pretty confident about my conversational English. One day, someone asked me, 'Are you from Tokyo?' He said this in an upper-class English accent and Tokyo sounded like this 'təʊkyəʊ'. I could not understand what he was saying! He must have thought that I was not too bright because he assumed that 'təʊkyəʊ' was a word that I would obviously understand – a Japanese word after all!

Now, these problems might never have occurred had I realized that the way the English pronounce certain letters is not the same as they are taught in Japan. I had thought that the 'O' sound was pronounced 'ɔ:' but actually English people tend to pronounce it as 'əʊ'. But that knowledge would probably not have been enough. In addition to the sound of the letter, there is the rhythm of the language (the accent and the intonation). Now, in English and Japanese the accents and intonations are quite different. Even with very clear pronunciation of the letters, if your rhythm is incorrect you might be misunderstood – or perhaps not even understood at all. That is why the Kawata Method also emphasizes the learning of the differences that exist in intonation and accent between English and Japanese.

(2) If you want to speak English well get the rhythm (accent and intonation) of English right.

These days, non-Japanese who appear on Japanese TV speak good Japanese. However, when I listen closely to the Japanese these speakers use, there is hardly anyone who really speaks the language well. The reason is because they cannot avoid speaking Japanese with their own linguistic rhythm. For instance, those who speak English as their mother tongue would say, 'Wat-**a**-shiwa Am-**e**-rica kar-**a** kimash-**i**- ta': they cannot avoid stressing a syllable of each word because it is a linguistic rule in English.

Then, how can a person whose mother tongue is English speak Japanese well? 'It's easy, speak Japanese flatly without your linguistic rhythm', you might say to the foreign Japanese-speaking person. It is not at all easy for someone to abandon the accent and intonation of his or her native language; to do so will actually take a considerable effort. In other words, there is the secret of a Japanese person becoming capable of speaking English well, it is the opposite problem to the foreign person not being able to speak Japanese well, just like the reverse side of a coin.

(3) Because you are Japanese, you have got to be able to speak English well!

You might be surprised if I tell you that the Japanese are born with the innate ability to speak English well. The reason that I say this is that Japanese is, in terms of sounds, a monotonous, flat language that does not have a noticeable rhythm in it. When one learns to speak a foreign language well, the most difficult part of doing so is to speak the language without one's own linguistic rhythm; in other words one has to hide one's own accent.

For instance, a French person trying to speak English well will never be able to do so if he or she speaks English with a French accent. The same could be said when an English person is trying to speak French well. So when a French or English person tries to learn the other's language, they have to start from 'minus' because they have noticeable rhythms in their respective languages. Whereas a Japanese person can start from 'zero', as it were, because Japanese does not have a prominent rhythm. In other words, because the Japanese speak a monotonous tongue, they have a head start for learning to speak any foreign language well, including English. In short, I might reiterate, 'Because you are Japanese, you have got to be able to speak English well! '

However, a Japanese person has always to bear in mind that unless he or she is thoroughly acquainted with those sounds of English 'f, l, r, v, θ, ð, æ, ʌ, ə, ɜ:, əʊ, etc.', which do not appear in Japanese, his or her English will become like that of Mr Aoki's (cf. Chapter 1, page 11) and will not make sense at all to the English ear.

• Different dialects of English

Is it only a few difficult letters and a new pattern of linguistic rhythms that stop you from speaking English well? Well, almost – but there is the question of dialect. The Kawata Method emphasises a strong, carefully pronounced Standard English, which will be recognised and understood internationally. While you will be understood, you might still experience problems in understanding what the other person is saying. One of the obvious ways in which this comes about is because the form of English that he, or she, is using is not Standard English. Dialects in English add to the richness of the language but they do make things difficult for the Japanese English learner.

(1) Sympathy that was not called for!

Having overcome many linguistic and educational barriers, I was admitted to the University of London to follow a postgraduate course. Although I was very confident in my English-speaking abilities, I could never converse easily with friends and acquaintances from African and Asian countries because of their heavy and (for me) difficult accents to understand.

At the beginning, I used to sympathize with them. I thought that it would be very difficult for them to follow a postgraduate course with the English skills that they possessed. One day, I was having lunch with Mr A., a student from Malaysia. I had noticed that he had a difficult accent to understand and I really felt quite sorry for him.

During lunch, I confided that I was only slowly getting accustomed to the rhythm of his English. I explained that I did not have a first degree from an English university and that it was extremely difficult to follow the course. No doubt, I said, 'it must be just as difficult for you as well'.

He paused, and spoke slowly in English that even I could not fail to understand. 'I understand that you are having difficulties, and you are quite right – you were not educated in the English language. I, on the other hand, have been educated in English from kindergarten all the way through this postgraduate course. I have also passed the English Bar examination and have practised for the last ten years as a barrister.'

I turned very red and felt really embarrassed. I had made a mistake. I had not recognized that he was an excellent English speaker who spoke in a non-Standard English dialect. He had great skills in the language and had no difficulty in following the course. It was simply that he spoke in a way that, while proper and acceptable, was unfamiliar to me. At this point, he smiled and said, 'I'm afraid that you will indeed have a hard time ahead because your first degree was in Japanese. That will make learning international law difficult for you.' And he was correct. I spent the next few years losing my confidence in my ability ever to speak English successfully and being constantly mystified by the legal jargon of the course.

After that, having had several similar experiences, I came to realize that 'there are various Englishes in the world'. In that when one gets used to their accents, one will realize how accurately they are using excellent English expressions.

However, in some areas and countries, English expressions are changing from the original ones. Therefore, they might be classified as different dialects of English rather than different Englishes.

(2) The English of the English, the English of the Americans
One day, when I was passing a kitchen in the Hall of Residence, from inside I heard the lively and cheerful voices of some students. So I peeped in and found some people in the middle of a tea party. As I knew one of them, I was soon asked to join them.

I was offered a cup of tea and was just about to take my first sip, when someone with a rather strong American accent exclaimed: 'Hot (hɑt), hot (hɑt), it's damn hot (its diyæm hɑt)! You'll burn your tongue (tiyæng)!' which I did not understand at all. Actually, he was kindly trying to warn me that the tea was very hot and that I should be careful not to burn my tongue. However, I was left wondering what he meant and was just dumbfounded. It later turned out that he came from Louisiana, one of the southern states in America. Up until then, I did have some American friends and felt quite accustomed to their accent but I was really stumped by his American English.

Now, as I said at the beginning of this chapter, American English seems to be more widely diffused than Standard English in some areas of the world, including Japan. This, to a degree, is understandable because of America's economic and military power. I feel somewhat annoyed as I still think that American English is one of the dialects of the English language, and that the English of England is Standard English. However, if we go back through the history of the English language, the relationship between Standard English and American English might become slightly clearer.

An American friend once told me that towards the end of the nineteenth century there was an attempt to create another language from English in the United States. He said with sarcasm: 'Luckily, it wasn't successful, consequently the Americans and the English can still communicate with each other, though not well enough.' There seems to be some traces of this attempt, which makes American English different from Standard English. As my friend from Louisiana demonstrated, they say 'Hot (hɑt)' in American English instead of 'Hot (hɔt)' in Standard English, which might be one of them.

In English, 'R' at the end of words is not pronounced, whereas it is pronounced in American English. Thus 'car (kɑ:)', 'door (dɔ:)', 'four (fɔ:)', etc. are pronounced without the 'R' sound at the end of the word, but are pronounced in American English as 'car (kɑ:r)', 'door (dɔ:r)', 'four (fɔ:r)', etc. As 'R' at the end of words is also pronounced in Ireland, the influence of about forty million Irish Americans in the US can be strongly felt there.

About thirty years ago, returning to Japan after a year's study in England, I looked through some one hundred English expressions with an

American friend. This friend understood about 90% of these expressions, but did not know or had never heard of the others. The interesting fact was that among the 90% of the expressions that he knew, many, while used contemporarily in America, were considered antiquated in England. This phenomenon can often be found in the linguistic world. It is said, for example, that some expressions used in the old capital city of Kyoto still remain in use in Tohoku Province, which is far from both Tokyo and Kyoto in the north of Japan.

(3) Using the Kawata 'R' you can talk to Americans.

I am talking to you about Standard English spoken in England. However, as previously noted, in Japan many people think that American English is English. As I am not an expert on American English, I will not be able to consider this subject in detail. Through my dealings with American people, especially when I was starting to speak English, there was a language barrier in my not understanding them. I would like to tell you how I was able to overcome it.

Although I do not intend to go into detail as to the differences between English and American English it might be useful if you know some further pronunciation differences between the two.

These are some examples of words which are pronounced 'ɔ' in English but 'ɑ' in American English:

hot, volleyball, God, rock, lock, etc.

Also, as mentioned earlier, 'R' at the end of words is not pronounced in English whereas it is pronounced in American English. The Kawata R will be useful so that you will be able to pronounce these words 'in the American way'. Try to pronounce words in the American way by using the Kawata R for:

four, car, paper, mother, father, brother, etc.

Above all, I found it extremely difficult to get my (ɜː) sound understood in talking to American people. Therefore, if I have to use a word with an (ɜː) sound in it when talking to Americans who are unfamiliar with the English, I pronounce it in the American manner using the Kawata R. With words such as 'first, third, bird, nurse, heard, etc.', Americans have difficulty understanding them if they are pronounced in the English way.

As an exercise, try to read the following sentence in (a) the Standard English manner, and then (b) in the American manner with the Kawata R:

'First, I've got to tell you, Mr Bird, I would like to see you at four-thirty tomorrow afternoon.'

(4) What will the future relationship be between English and American English?

The United States is presently the most powerful country militarily and economically in the world. If there is an inferiority complex in the United States it will be their language, which is still being borrowed from the mother country, England. Will there, therefore, be a movement, as there was a hundred years ago, to create another language? I do not think that there will be such a movement in the United States, for a while at least.

I think that one of the reasons why there was a movement to create another language in the past was because the British government did not make any attempt to save Ireland during the Potato Famine of 1845–47. It seems that the emotional complications between England (Britain) and Ireland caused people to stay away from Britain and to consider creating a language different from English.

Recently, the Prime Minister of Britain, Mr Tony Blair, officially apologised to Ireland for having taken a wrong policy during the Potato Famine in Ireland. This will help alleviate the deep, 150-year-old hatred felt by the Irish towards the English. This will improve the relationship between Ireland and Britain and also contribute to a better relationship between Britain and the United States.

CHAPTER 6

☐ Harmony is everything in Japanese society

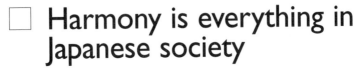

Why recession? Can Japan recover from the recession?

IN THIS CHAPTER, it will be observed how capitalism which was born in England (Britain) was accepted into Japan after World War II. It will be also explained that the Kawata Method was born out of realization that the Japanese race is a rather unique and peculiar one whose language is highly visual. And the Japanese national characteristics, which have for a long time been enshrined in mystery will be elucidated. Japan should be proud of its national character of 'Ideological Cooperativism', upon which social form for the next generation of human beings is to be based. Japan will recover from the recession if the Japanese realize how important it is for them to get themselves fully acquainted with the English language, which is vocal and different from their own, which is visual.

- ● What is capitalism?
  Something that spread from England to the world

Capitalism was born out of Materialism in eighteenth-century England, where individualism was dominantly prevalent, and spread from there to the rest of the world. Adam Smith (1723–90) wrote in his book, *The Wealth of Nations*, 'The development of society should be best led by the free competition of people based on their egoistic needs.'

Carl Marx (1818–83), in his *Dialectic Materialism Theory*, advocates: 'A capitalist society is a process of development of human societies, which will be replaced with a socialist society by revolution. The socialist society will be again replaced by a communist society where there are no classes of people, which is the same as the peaceful, non-competitional society of the primitive age, but it has been dialectically developed and refined.'

About thirty years ago, when I was a student in Tokyo, student movements were vigorously going on everywhere, and there were quite a few pseudo Marxists around me. Although I was rather indifferent to politics, I often got involved in political debates.

One day, a close friend of mine, who was at a University in Kyoto, came to see me after a long period apart. He had been greatly influenced by Marxism, and as I was more inclined towards capitalism, he tried to entice me into a philosophical debate about communism. So I posed the following question: 'There are two men in the desert. There is only enough food for one. If they share it they will both die. What should they do?'

He insisted: 'Human beings are different from ordinary animals. They have reason. So they will try to share it all the way to the very last morsel.' So I persisted: 'Human beings are also animals. While they have reason they might share it. But what would happen if they lost that reason?' He replied: 'Such a situation is rather unthinkable and would not occur in this civilized world of ours.' He might be right, but faced with a predicament like that, I think that they would fight over the food.

The person who won the food, 'won life' and must have thought, the more food he had the longer he would be able to survive. That food in our modern society is 'money'. For with money, one can gain almost anything including food. That is, 'there is a competitive essence in human beings dictated by the eating instinct.' I might make bold to say that Marx seems to have always based his theories on rational human beings. In other words, I would think that competition is an essence of human beings, and that capitalism reflects that essence.

And the fight over money is the competition in the capitalist market. Today, by all means, they do not kill each other. It is conducted within certain rules. However, one might lose one's life indirectly by being defeated in the competition. For instance, one might commit suicide following bankruptcy. Thus, 'Taking away from each other is the capitalist society'.

In this capitalist society, an individual can do whatever he/she wants as long as he/she does not hurt others. Capitalism, which was born out of individualism in England, has since spread throughout the rest of the world.

• England is a mature capitalist society

I thought that by staying with an English family and going to an English-language school, I would soon become proficient in English. Thus, I went over to England and stayed in a town called Ramsgate in Kent. My English family was a rather peculiar one. It was comprised of a young wife and her six-year-old daughter. The husband was seldom at home.

Although I spoke almost no English, I tried to communicate with the family members in English. Or rather, like a spoilt Japanese child, I self-righteously decided that the English family was my family in England, and that they would teach me some English.

The day after I arrived there, as the Japanese customarily do, I gave the family members gifts from Japan. As they received them, they were kind and tried to communicate with me. I spoke very faltering English, however, and had to use my dictionary every five seconds on that day. But, that was it! After that, the family did not teach me a single word of English. On top of that, the wife was very strict about table manners. In those days, I would eat soup noisily, and she would tell me off severely. Today, oddly enough, I am grateful to the 'demon' young wife for that lesson.

Meanwhile, I made friends with some Japanese students at the school and we soon started exchanging stories about each other's families. It turned out that most of the families did not teach the students English, as had been expected, nor did they take them out or treat them as family members despite the fact that this was mentioned in the school's brochure. From the point of view of the families, it was understandable: they were getting paid to provide the students with room and board, not for communicating with individuals who hardly spoke English.

It appeared that all of the English families were more or less the same. Even so, mine seemed to be the worst, so I asked the school to change my English family. As the secretary of the school was a friend of my English family, it took quite some time until she finally relocated me with another family.

This time, it was an old couple and even worse than before; once again it was the wife who was unfriendly. On the day I moved to the second family, when I was studying late at night in my room, all of a sudden, without a knock, the door swung open and the landlady rushed into my room. She turned off the lamp on the desk which was the only light in the room. I was very surprised and said: 'What's going on?' She replied angrily: 'Your school is not paying for the electricity you are using at this time of the day. Electricity is very expensive here.'

I stopped short of swearing at her. With my broken English, I managed to say: 'As I have to work late at night in the room, I'll pay you directly for the electricity which is not covered by the school. How about that?' She was very pleased with the suggestion and so, from then on I was able to use the light. I have never met anyone who became proficient in English thanks to being with an English family. Or rather, we should not expect them to treat us as their family members. In this mature capitalist society of England, each individual has been permeated with capitalism. In short: 'Without money one doesn't open one's mouth, if one opens one's mouth one demands money.'

● The American people
(The national character of the American people)

The United States became independent from Britain in 1776. You might say everyone knows it. I would say not everyone, particularly amongst the young people in Japan.

Now, what is the difference between the Americans and the English, both of whom derive from Britain? I think that there is some kind of 'cooperativism' in the United States which differs from the English individualism. In the process of constructing a country, the US has overcome many difficulties.

Various ethnic peoples got together and worked towards forming a nation in the US. It seems that in the process, a sense of cooperation was born which I call 'cooperativism' in the United States. The birth of this cooperativism was made possible because there was such an abundance of land and natural resources in the US. In other words, without fighting, the Americans were able to acquire land and cultivate undeveloped land. (Of course, we should not forget the Civil War or the painful fighting with the Native Americans.)

Above all, the most outstanding feature of the Americans is their 'positive thinking'. They have been able to develop it because their ancestors went over to the United States and succeeded in creating a better life for themselves.

The students who stayed with American families have a different opinion from the ones who stayed with English families. As they have worked together in forging a nation they are kind to foreign people and are ready to accept them into their families.

On the other hand, it is said that the Americans are somewhat simplistic. For instance, when there was a war between Israel and the

Arab countries in 1973 I was in Oxford. It came to Japan as a great shock, for the Japanese Economy was heavily dependant upon the oil from the Arab countries. In *The Times* newspaper at that time, a high-ranking American diplomat was quoted as saying: 'We saw the weak point of the Japanese economy. It will be the end of Japan.' On the contrary, in the same paper an English goverment official was quoted as saying: 'We have seen the revival of Japan after the Second World War. She will be back on her feet again.' I was rather impressed with that comment.

- The Japanese national character
  Harmony is everything in Japanese society
  'Ideological cooperativism'

When I was in a pub during my first visit I was repeatedly told by a barman that the Japanese were inscrutable. At that time, I did not know the meaning of the word. Even after having looked it up in the dictionary I still did not understand why the Japanese were inscrutable to the English people. Living in England, I was gradually beginning to understand that the things the Japanese do and consider to be right and common sense were inscrutable to the English.

So, let us consider how the Japanese National characteristics were formed, including their 'inscrutability'. Though I touched upon the Japanese National Character in Chapter 1 'Vocal Language (English) and Visual Language (Japanese)', I will make bold to repeat it as it constitutes the core of my theory.

Thus, when we talk about the Japanese National Character there are two important factors to remember. One of them is that from time immemorial they have been engaged in agriculture and living in small village communities. As they were agricultural people, they were tied down to the land and were unable to move freely. The other is that they are islanders and have always been isolated from the rest of the world. The Japanese have been pursuing their lives in village units throughout history. Whenever natural disasters occurred, like earthquakes, typhoons or famines, they were united and fought against them as a village. Out of all this, there were born various Japanese national characteristics.

First, one had to work as hard as the others and to be strictly disci-plined in the village community. One spoke as little as possible and silently worked hard. These things had been kept dreadfully well, because if a villager was once ousted from his/her village, he/she would be facing potential death in a country surrounded by water. In other words, once ostracised, the villager had no place to go, as one would be considered a trouble-maker in all other villages. In Japan, where there is no neighbouring country to escape to, 'Mulahachibu (ostracism)' was the same as being sentenced to death. So villagers worked hard so as not to be ousted from their villages. They kept their mouths shut as much as possible, for they knew perfectly well that if they voiced an ill-considered opinion, it would be the end of their lives. There is an old saying in Japan: 'Out of the mouth comes evil.' This 'evil' could lead to Mulahachibu.

Therefore, above their individual interest, villagers thought first of the interest of the village as a whole. That is, they valued the harmony of the village community more than the interest of the individual. Out of all this, cooperativism like a national character was born in Japan.

Let us see, therefore, if some Japanese characteristics agree with the above.

a. The Japanese are said to be kind: Living in a small village community, if you are kind to others they will be kind to you in return when you are in trouble. 'Kindness is not for others, but for yourself,' is an old saying in Japan.

b. 'ishindenshin' (telepathy): Reading each other's minds. The expression originally comes from Buddhism. Without speaking or writing, people read each other's mind. When one lived in a small community where they valued the harmony of the village most and spoke little, it was not difficult to imagine what the other villagers had in mind.

c. One does not disgrace oneself: One of the worst things one could do was to disgrace oneself. If one did so, it would be difficult to stay on in the village. It could be a matter of life and death.

d. To efface oneself or kill oneself: In order to maintain the harmony in the village, one avoided expressing oneself at all costs.

e. To this day, the Japanese do not like arguments: In a community where the harmony of the village is valued above all else, an argument which is likely to disrupt the harmony is disliked, and avoided at all costs.

f. The Japanese are on good terms with their neighbours: Not only with their neighbours, but also with everyone so as to stay in the village.

g. The Japanese are always ready with a smile: To foreign people it is an inscrutable smile. For the Japanese, it is a sign of them having no hostility.

h. The Japanese have a strong sense of responsibility: One has to carry out one's village duties and responsibilities. Otherwise one could be expelled from the village.

i. The Japanese keep promises: Once a promise is made, one has to keep it in a village community. Otherwise one would be expelled from the village.

j. *Kamikaze Tokkotai*: Towards the end of the Second World War, the Japanese were desperately fighting against the Allied Forces. Thereupon, they decided to form a suicide squad of fighters. The fighters, carrying large quantities of bombs, crashed into enemy battle-ships. They were called *Kamikaze-Tokkotai*. How were the pilots able to do such a thing? I read their letters and diaries. They firmly believed that if they carried out their duties, their lovers, parents, sisters, brothers and the whole of Japan would be saved, and hence the harmony of the country would be kept.

k. '*seppuku or halakili*': This is a means of committing suicide for samulai (warriors). One disembowled oneself with a sword. How were they able to do so? It would be difficult to generalize, as this act was performed under various circumstances. For instance, if a samulai made a crucial blunder in his work, he could be ordered to commit halakili by his lord. He did so in the belief that his wife, parents and children would be saved from ostracism, and hence the harmony of the household would be kept.

There are quite a few more national characteristics of the Japanese to be discussed. Let us sum up what we have covered so far. What the villagers valued most was the harmony of the village community. It was valued more than 'materials' or 'money'. Though villagers did not speak a lot, they were able to read each other's minds. That is to say, they were not ruled by material possessions or money. They came to be ruled by an idea called 'harmony'. Thereupon, I call this characteristic of the villagers, or rather the character of the Japanese, 'Ideological Cooperativism'.

● Japan's recovery after the war

Having lost the war, 'the disgraced Japanese' desperately worked hard. For a resourceless country like Japan, the time of peace was best, as she could obtain essential materials from wherever she wanted. The Japanese are, by nature, a non-aggressive and peace-loving people.

Now, how was capitalism, which was born out of individualism in England, accepted into Japan after the war? Japanese companies, whether they were large or small, seemed to have the form of a village. Each employee worked hard for his company and for his community. Most of the employees would work for their companies until their retirement age. The collection of all those companies is Japan. The employees worked hard for their companies and the companies worked hard for Japan. Meanwhile, in order to maintain a high quality workforce, the country put up a high standard of education for the people. Even though the Japanese were diligent enough, they vied with one another to obtain higher academic results to work for better companies.

As a result, Japan has become one huge company, sometimes referred to as 'Japan Inc'. The Japan Enterprise Limited, vested with Ideological Cooperativism, kept on winning versus other countries in the capitalist market.

On the other hand, it was difficult for other countries to penetrate the Japanese Market, as the Japanese had retained the rule of the village community throughout history, not to accept outsiders (someone expelled from another village) into their community. So it did not take long for Japan to become the second biggest economic power in the world.

● Why recession?
Because the Japanese stopped being Japanese

After the war, Japan worked frantically. Through commercial exchanges with the materialistic individualist countries, Japan started questioning its way of life. She had been constantly criticized about the size of her trade surplus at the summit of the seven largest economic powers as it was then. She was told by the rest of the world that she was overworking and that Japan was a nation of workaholics. She took those criticisms seriously.

What made Japan worry most was the possibility of being expelled from the group of the seven economic powers. That is, *Mulahachibu* (ostracism); she was very self-conscious and afraid of being ostracized by the world community. Therefore, Japan started destroying the core of its national character. The slogan, 'Let's make Japan rest!' was well disseminated throughout the country. They stopped being diligent. The Compulsory School Education Board also created a slogan, 'Education at Leisure!' School children started to lack discipline and neglected public morals. Japan as a whole stopped being Japanese. Cyclists selfishly started cycling on the right-hand side – the wrong side of the road, as if to say: 'One is free to do anything one wants.' Vested with this slogan 'Education at Leisure!', school teachers were forced to reverse their educational principles and adopt a more relaxed approach.

At this point, having worked hard for forty years since the war, the Japanese must have thought that they needed a break. But the capitalist competition continued. It was just like rowing upstream; once they stopped advancing, they would be taken back by the stream. They were not able to stay where they stopped rowing.

On top of that, as China and Russia had begun participating in the capitalist competition, Japan Inc. sustained a major blow. Chinese penetration into the Japanese market, in particular, dealt a deadly blow to some traditional Japanese industries.

Then, whatever the Japanese did had the opposite effect to what was intended. Secret meetings were convened so as not to show the difference of opinions of the village community. Any difference of opinion was throughly ironed out and the villagers always reached the consensus of their opinions. This was the wisdom of the Japanese. But the interpretation of these meanings was negatively changed into '*dangoh* (collusion)', '*naleai* (conspiracy)' and '*yuchaku* (collusion)' between the public and the private sectors), which accelerated the recession of the Japanese economy.

• In order to overcome the recession, discipline and order have to be restored

Let us look back on those days when the Japanese economy was doing well. We had the 'monolithic' union.

What 'Education at Leisure' is aiming for is 'A Free Society at Leisure', and not 'A Disordered, Ruleless Society'. First, I would like to see cyclists ride on the correct side of the road, the left-hand side, which will be a good start for getting back discipline and order to society. I would like teachers and policemen to diligently make them thoroughly abide by the law. It will not only reduce the number of traffic accidents involving cyclists, but will also make them realize that there is discipline and order in society.

The fact that cyclists abide by the traffic rules and ride on the left-hand side will trigger off the movement of getting back discipline and order throughout Japan. They should teach children at school that they must be proud of the Japanese national character of diligence and their law-abiding nature, and that Japanese value harmony of the community most and are the most peace-loving nation in the world.

● If Japanese society loses its harmony, and continues ingratiating itself with the West, Japan will soon disappear from the world

Most people in capitalist societies are materialistic and are freely pursuing their economic activities. That is what capitalism is all about. Economic wars are fiercely being fought in the capitalist market. The wars appear to be fought between countries, however, they are in fact wars between individual workers in different countries. Whether a country can be successful in the capitalist market or not very much depends on the quality of its manpower and education.

Why had Japan been successful in the capitalist market? Because there had not been a country like Japan before. The Japanese who had Ideological Cooperativism, which was born out of the village community, were diligent, law abiding and able to kill themselves in order to maintain the harmony and interest of the community. I have used a rather old and fearful expression 'to kill oneself (that is to say, to sacrifice oneself)'. This was the very Japanese virtue which foreigners had not been familiar with. In other words, the Japanese had been Japanese. That is why they had been winning the economic wars.

In the post-war years, the Japanese worked like hell to catch up with the other capitalist countries. Some forty years later, when Japan realized where she was, there was no one else there except for herself. What was waiting for her was not praise and applause but a storm of criticisms – 'Isn't it a free world ?' she said to herself. 'They (the US, Britain, and all the other economic powers) say I am selfish because I'm stealing the show. But I don't want to be ousted from the capitalist society (*Mulahachibu*). So I'd better do as I am told.' So she stopped working hard and began neglecting rules and public morals. On top of that, a newly-born enterprising country, Russia, and a hard-working country, China (just like Japan right after the war), entered the capitalist market. While Japan was being taken aback, she became the most backward pupil amongst them and entered an endless tunnel of recession which seems to have no way out.

Having lost herself in the maze of a recession, Japan has now lost confidence in herself and is losing sight of herself today. Instead, she is now ingratiating herself with materialistic capitalist countries. For instance, 'the yard-stick' called 'Global Standard', which the materialistic capitalist countries came up with, could not be applied in its full extent to Japan. Of course, because she has chosen to stay within the capitalist system, she has to abide by the rules and regulations of the system.

However, with her national character of Ideological Cooperativism, Japan has the basic social structure for the next generation of human beings. As her society values the harmony of the community most, she can conversely put to them that there is something more important than money in our lives, namely harmony in the world, in other words, world peace. She should assume world leadership in achieving this.

Now, almost every day on TV and in the media, economists and politicians are debating how to deal with the recession. Most of them use cheap trickery, and have not got a deep enough grasp of the problem. It seems to me that their way of dealing with the recession might be effective in the short term but not at all effective in the long run. That is to say, unless the Japanese start being Japanese again, the recession essentially cannot be solved.

Now, there are various kinds of races and social structures in the world. Each ethnic group has a different concept of happiness. Certainly, it is to satisfy the desire for the materialistic needs of a capitalist society. In order to do so, it often approves of wars. Well, wars themselves might be acceptable for a capitalist society – however, on this earth of ours, there are people who prefer 'spiritual satisfaction to materialistic satisfaction (peace to war)'. For those who live in a capitalist society, it might be high time to stop enforcing our values on less industrialized countries and start thinking about 'what happiness is all about'.

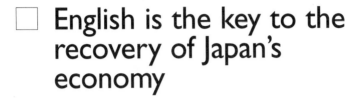 English is the key to the recovery of Japan's economy

The role of Japanese women in the 21st century

HAVE YOU REALIZED that English is a vocal language in comparison with Japanese? No, not yet!? Then, please read this chapter. You will realize that speaking English for native English speakers is, to use a metaphor, 'like fighting with real swords'. I would like the Japanese reader also to realize that for them speaking English is directly related to their economic activities. In no uncertain terms, I would like you to understand why you not only have to be able to speak English but speak it properly.

● 'English! You've got to be able to speak it.'

How was language born? For instance, there is an object. One gives it a name in 'sound'. People start using 'the sound' to each other to relate to that material, and therefore they have a common recognition about it. Little by little, they name things around them and use these words with each other, and from there an action called 'speaking' started and language was born.

Why, then, did 'speaking' come first? Because the action of speaking is to transfer sounds between people. 'Sound' is invisible and intangible. In fact, 'sound' is a material called a sound wave. One feels the material in one's body. In other words, the action of speaking is that one transfers an object to the person being spoken to. This is another indication that human beings are materialistic. Human beings were able to evolve separately from ordinary animals because they started speaking and walking on two legs.

Well, as mentioned above, the action of speaking is a materialistic transfer and the most natural and important part of the linguistic activities of human beings. It reinforces the fact that human beings have an instinct to eat and can only survive by obtaining food (a material) and consuming it. Human beings are indeed materialistic creatures as you might recall from the story about two lost men in the desert in the previous chapter.

What are the characteristics of English then? English is a language which was born in England. The English were originally nomads on the continent of Europe, moving from one place to another, verbally and skilfully establishing good human relations with the people wherever they went, and they became very good at diplomacy. For them 'to speak' was a very important means of life; therefore, because of their racial characteristics, English has become a vocal language and developed more complicated sounds and a wider tonal range than Japanese, distinguishing meanings of words by sound or by intonation (ban-van, law-raw, etc.).

The English are very cautious about uttering the sound 'Sorry' because they sometimes have to be very accountable for that sound. That is, if someone hit your car in England, although it was not your fault at all, being Japanese, out of politeness you would say 'Sorry'. At that time, the other party would think that you would take full responsibility for the accident.

Another example, 'You have my word !' is an expression meaning 'I promise! (The contract has been completed!)' and it even has the same effect as a written contract. These examples show that the English value 'sounds' very much. On the other hand, there is an expression in Japanese 'A verbal promise is not dependable!' which illustrates well the fact that Japanese and English view 'the action of speaking' differently in their respective languages.

Incidentally, if I may digress slightly, Chinese characters are idiograms, therefore one might think Chinese is a typical visual language. However, considering how much the Chinese value 'sounds' in their language, it should rather be classified as a vocal language. There are some sounds in Chinese that many English people cannot pronounce. It proves how complicated the Chinese language is in terms of sounds. The Chinese seldom say 'Sorry!', for they know 'that sound (that word)' might change their destiny. Why did not communism take root in China? Because the Chinese had an individualistic national character deep down in themselves, which opposes the communist ideology based on 'Ideological Cooperativism'.

Today, so many are permeated with capitalism in the mature capitalist society of England, where it appears to be the trend of the age that 'Sound Is Money'. That is, 'Unless one is paid money one does not open one's mouth, and if one opens one's mouth one demands money.'

The English have a completely different attitude from the Japanese towards 'speaking'. In short, it might be extreme to say but, 'It's not enough that you can read and write English. It is meaningless, if you can't speak it.'

● Japan can take a leading role at the summit of the major eight economic nations.

Every year, when I see the Japanese Premier at a summit conference on TV, I am disappointed by his lack of confidence. I seem to witness this, irrespective of the state of the Japanese Economy. I am sure everyone else in Japan is hoping that as our representative at these summits, the Prime Minister will behave in a manner that is more natural and dignified. It is because I love Japan so much that I have given my opinions so candidly. But in fact, I understand the psychology of the Japanese Premier very well.

Japanese culture regards discretion and modesty as virtues and rejects self-assertion. It is only natural for the Japanese, brought up in such an environment, to get puzzled at a situation where unless one is assertive, one's very existence is ignored. However, on reflection, Japan is being obliged to compromise its national character, at least in relation to the outside world.

The Free World Leaders are materialistic vocal language people. As long as Japan lives in this materialistically civilized society brought about by them, she has to participate in 'the taking away of materials (money, capital, etc.) from each other' and has to have a full command over the English language, which has now become the lingua franca in the international community. For the World Leaders, the summit conference is a battlefield where they may claim their own nations' profits (gains and returns). Though these leaders are superficially gentle and peaceful, they are fighting desperately at the summit.

Japan has to learn an important lesson from the current recession. That is, for the materialistic vocal language people, including native English people, 'speaking English' is more than a sheer means of communicating. It is not only transferring sounds from one person to another, but it is, to use a metaphor, like 'fighting with real swords'. It can be explained from materialism (human beings are materialistic) that sound is a material (like food, money, etc.) which is necessary to maintain life. The Japanese have to take mastering the English language more seriously. In international law, a party to a treaty is regarded as having given its consent at the conclusion if it keeps silent. In other words, a party which does not utter a sound is considered as having discarded 'life', as if to say, 'Please do as you like'.

On the other hand, the Japanese language has been developed differently in the village community. Once a villager was ousted from a village, in a country surrounded by water, what would wait for him next was 'death'. Therefore, one spoke as little as possible and tried not to make a slip of the tongue. As a result, Japanese became a visual language putting more emphasis on writing and reading than on speaking.

How then can the Japanese (a visual language people) speak English (a vocal language) well? First, please read Chapter 2 of this book, then become fully acquainted with those sounds of English which do not exist in Japanese in Chapter 3. At this point, your English could be understood throughout the world. Then read Chapter 4, 'Because you are Japanese, you've got to be able to speak English well!' After reading, you will understand that the Japanese are born with an innate ability to speak English well. To be able to speak a foreign language well, one has to master the rhythm of the language. The more noticeable rhythm one has in one's own language, the more difficult it is to learn another language. As the Japanese do not have a noticeable rhythm in their language, as soon as they have acquired the rhythm of English, they should be able to speak English well.

During my postgraduate course at London University, I recorded all the classes with a tape recorder and wrote down every word after listening to the tapes. My tutor was a Cantabrigian who spoke excellent English. It often took me more than fifteen hours to listen to a tape and to transcribe the words. I was repeatedly voicing the words at the same time as I listened to the tape and wrote them down.

About two years later, I sought medical attention at a hospital for the flu. I somehow got involved in a dispute with the doctor there. Thereupon, suddenly he said with a sober look on his face: 'I'd better stop it, as I will never be able to win over you in this argument. You are an excellent orator. You must be a barrister.' 'Why do you say so?' I asked him. 'My elder brother is also a barrister. You speak exactly in the same way as he does,' he answered. I was unconsciously speaking in the same way as my tutor who was also a barrister. After that incident, I purposely imitated his English. Thanks to him, I made rapid progress in learning English; however, I recall it was rather embarrassing sometimes when I met him.

'Imitation is the sincerest form of flattery', is an English saying. Whereas one has a rather negative attitude towards imitation in Japan.

As already noted, I mastered the rhythm of English by imitating my tutor's English. The best way to master the rhythm of English is by repeatedly listening to good English and repeating it aloud. Find someone who speaks good English and imitate that person's English. In doing so, you are demonstrating your respect for that person. However, before doing so, please make sure that you have mastered those sounds of English which do not exist in Japanese. Otherwise, you might speak English with a good rhythm, but it might not make much sense to the English listener.

• Japanese women will be world leaders in the twenty-first century

Women make up half of the world's population. I have long thought that women are more materialistic than men. I assume this is because women are vested with the most important task of human beings, to preserve the human race. That is, in order to perpetuate the human race, women are more determined than men to survive at any cost. It is widely believed that women are better at learning languages (especially the spoken part) than men. This could also be explained by the fact that women are more materialistic than men, since sound becomes a material called a sound wave and it is felt in their body. If you are a female reader of this book and have not thought about it, then 'Better late than never!' If you start learning English now, you will soon discover your aptitude for this skill.

How about Japanese Women then? I think they are definitely more materialistic than Japanese men. On top of that, having been born and brought up in Japan they are vested with 'Ideological Cooperativism'. Or rather, they are the ones who have kept the household and have made the ideological country Japan. Japanese women will become more and more active in the world since they are good at English (materialistic), they are considerate and value the harmony of the community most (ideological). I think that Japanese women do embody Ideological Cooperativism best.

I think that Japan will be able to play a leading role as a mediator at the summit of the eight biggest economic powers. If the Japanese participants learn English using the Kawata Method, they will be able to speak correct English. Outwardly, the fact that they have become proficient in English will make the West think that the Japanese have started taking the English language seriously and that they mean business. Inwardly, it will give the Japanese the confidence whereby they will be able to come into contact with foreign people naturally. Given the Japanese national character which values harmony above all, Japan will be able to play a significant role as mediator. Then, the Japanese representative at the summit might be a Japnanese woman, in that she speaks English well and is fully acquainted with the Japanese National Character. I, therefore, assert that Japanese women will be world leaders in the twenty-first century.

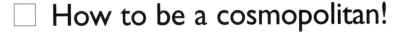 How to be a cosmopolitan!

IN THIS CHAPTER, I would like to talk about how a Japanese person could become a cosmopolitan. In order to become a cosmopolitan, it is advisable that he or she should get himself/herself fully acquainted with his/her own language and culture first.

Later in the chapter, the international nature of Rotary International, which is currently engaged in various activities around you, will be discussed, in that the moving experiences Rotarians might encounter through their activities will be doubled or tripled by directly talking to their fellow Rotarians in English.

● How to be a cosmopolitan!

(1) Irrespective of your age, you can speak English

A cosmopolitan is not someone who blindly absorbs foreign cultures, nor someone who makes frequent trips abroad and uses an excessive number of foreign words in speaking his/her own language (Japanese). However, I am not against the idea of young people making contact with foreign cultures nor learning English or other foreign languages.

As I noted earlier, I was almost twenty-three years old after my third year at university in Tokyo when I was first sent to England to study English for a year. The reason why I chose to go to England then was that I thought in order to be able to compare Japanese culture with that of the English, I should at least finish my general culture course at my own university and establish myself as a Japanese individual. Secondly, I placed the university education as the place to find my true potential, so while I was at university, by studying English in England I hoped that I would be able to know what I should do after graduation.

Well, up until the age of twenty-three, as I spoke only Japanese, I was promptly baptised in English at Victoria Station in London. You might recall (cf. Chapter I) that I was not able to get a ticket for my destination called 'Ramsgate'. This baptism must have been the realization which finally led to the birth of the Kawata Method of Learning English Conversation. In other words, as I spoke nothing but Japanese, I had to realize that there were some sounds in English which did not exist in Japanese, and that in order to be able to speak English, I had to acquire those sounds. I also realized that whereas Japanese was an intonationless, flat language, English was 'a vocal language' with a rising and falling intonation.

It was quite possible, because I was first exposed to English rather late, in my early twenties, that I might have been able to establish a method of learning English conversation logically. As a result, I was able to come up with the Kawata Method, whereby one can learn conversational English useful all over the world, in a short period of time, and regardless of one's age, without resorting too much to the limited number of native English teachers in Japan.

(2) Saved by Judo

Though I spoke no English when I started learning English in Ramsgate, Kent, I did manage to make some friends. It was thanks to Judo, which I started learning when I was a child. It was in the early 1970s that Judo became a recognized sport in the Olympics, however, among the ordinary people in England it was still one of the Oriental wonders where a tiny man would easily throw a big man.

There happened to be a self-proclaimed middle-weight Judo Champion from Italy at my English school, and he asked me to have a match with him. The rumour soon spread throughout the school that we were going to have the match in the school yard the following week. There were many spectators in the school yard on the day. They were waiting for an international Judo match between an Italian Judo champion and a Japanese Judo man. At last the match started, ten seconds . . . twenty seconds elapsed. Decisively, I used my favourite throw on him. My throw was a success and my opponent went flying.

Because of this victory I gained many fans and friends. One of them was Mr Y. from Switzerland. He unexpectedly offered to take me on a one-month tour to Switzerland in his car.

Judo also saved my life on a few occasions. One day, I was walking in a department store with an English teacher, Mr Thompson from Oxford.

He and I were taking the staircase from the fourth floor to the third floor. I was wearing shoes with high heels, and one of my heels somehow became caught, and I fell head first down the staircase about three metres below onto a landing. Imagine diving into a swimming pool, or in the same way diving down an entire flight of stairs in your house.

Fortunately, however, I was able to fall onto the landing without hitting any of the steps on my way. During the split second that I was in the air, I clearly remember measuring the space on the landing and calculating which break fall I should use: 'diving' or 'forward spinning'. I came to the conclusion that I should use forward spinning, as the landing was not big enough for a diving one. And in the next instance, I was standing on my feet and brushing the dust off my trousers.

Mr Thompson saw the fall from beginning to end, and was amazed that I was apparently unhurt and on my feet within a second afterwards. After the incident, I was told that he would often dine out on the story. As for me, I still, much to their reluctance, constantly instruct my daughters by saying: 'What counts most in Judo is to get yourself fully acquainted with break falls.'

In 1977, I was admitted to a post-graduate course at London University. What was waiting for me again there was Judo. This time I was appointed as the captain of my Judo Club. Apart from me, everyone else in the Club was English. A couple of American exchange students joined later. I did not want for English conversation every day.

(3) Sports and music are international lingua franca

I also discerned I had a certain talent which I did not know I had. One day, several Japanese students got together in my room and wanted to have 'sushi'. In those days there were only a few Japanese restaurants in London, which were all high class, so we poor students could not afford to go. Therefore, as I had an electric kettle for cooking rice given to me by my Singaporean friend, they said I should make some 'sushi'.

We got some raw fish from a nearby Japanese food shop. So I pretended to be a professional sushi cook making rice balls, and to my surprise they all came out fine, so I earned a reputation for being a good sushi chef. After practising for a couple of months making rice balls, I was able to make a hundred rice balls in twenty minutes. So, I also diffused Japanese sushi culture amongst the other students in the hall of residence.

However, after returning to Japan, I was showing off my rice ball-making skills, when my father asked: 'What were you doing over there in England?' I was rather embarrassed and had to convince him that I was studying harder than I was making sushi rice balls.

Here is another story from the hall of residence. One day, the Warden of the Hall asked me to come to his room. As I was then the president of the Japanese Society in the Hall he asked me if the Japanese Society could put on an event which would introduce something of Japanese culture. I took this back to the other members of the Society. They said, 'Yes, let's do it.' We started preparing for it.

We were also asked to cook Japanese food for about a hundred guests. We decided to prepare 'sukiyaki' for them. Unfortunately, there were no female members in the Japanese Society at that time, so we were left with no choice but to prepare it ourselves. It was not authentic sukiyaki, but thanks to the seasoning ingenuity of Prof. Takachio of Tokyo University of Foreign Languages, it was surprisingly delicious.

And now the show started. First, as I played the guitar, I sang some modern Japanese folk songs. Then we put on a Judo Demonstration which was executed well. Finally, we presented a skit depicting a middle-aged Japanese couple.

As we were short of people able to contribute, I had to be in the play as well. I was in a cold sweat all the time, but we somehow got through it. After all the performances, all the members of the Japanese Society stood on the stage in front of the audience and in celebration of the show's success we performed 'tejime (synchronized hand clapping)'. Although we were only six or seven people, the clapping was loud and beautifully executed, highlighting the splendour of Japanese culture, and fully compensating for a few clumsy moments during the show.

Now it is often said that sports and music are international lingua franca. I have thought so on many occasions in the past. The readers of this book probably enjoy various sports and have various specialities. If you are acquainted with sports and music which are international lingua franca, you can claim to be a cosmopolitan. As the twenty-first century has already begun, whether one likes it or not, one often hears the word 'cosmopolitan', and one has to know what a real cosmopolitan is in this ever-shrinking world.

A real cosmopolitan is, I think, a person who can read and write his/her own language well, who knows what his/her language is, and has knowledge and a good command of English whereby he/she can communicate his/her own culture to foreign people.

In the hope that you will become a real cosmopolitan and that this book will be useful in helping you to achieve it, I proceed to the next section where the cosmopolitan nature of the Rotary Club will be discussed.

• My thanks to the Rotary Club for the 'moving moments'

(1) Rotary Club (International) is an entrance to International Society

Rotary Club was started in 1905 by a lawyer called Paul Harris with his three friends in Chicago. As of June, 2004, there were 31,936 clubs in 166 countries in the world. In Japan, there were 2,336 clubs in 34 Districts. The number of Rotarians (members of Rotary Club are called Rotarians) as of that date worldwide totalled 1,219,532 of whom 104,019 were Japanese Rotarians.

The object of Rotary is to 'Serve Society'. Each Rotarian is a professional in his/her work and serves society through his/her profession. Rotarians throughout the world are united in the ideal of service, they are engaged in the advancement of international understanding, goodwill and peace through a world fellowship of business and professional people.

In principle, there is a rule of 'one profession one member' in each Rotary Club, that is, only one person from one profession is invited to join each Rotary Club. However, for instance, if three medical doctors wished to join the same Rotary Club, they would be able to do so by subdividing their profession; one of them could join as a paediatrician, another as a surgeon and the third as a gynaecologist.

An interesting aspect of Rotary is that once you have joined, you automatically also become a member of Rotary International through membership of your own Rotary Club. Thus, if you were unable to attend your own club's regular meeting, (most of the clubs meet once a week), you are able to attend any Rotary Club's regular meeting anywhere in the world. It is as if you had attended your own club. This is called 'make-up'. Twelve years ago, because of my work, I was posted to England for three months. During my stay there I attended different clubs' regular meetings every week and did 'make-up'. At that time, it was my great pleasure to attend various clubs' regular meetings. In short, 'Rotary Club is an entrance to International Society'.

(2) My admittance to Rotary Club (Rotary International)

My late father, who was also a Rotarian, used to speak with pride about the nature of Rotary International. When I was thinking of contributing to society through my profession, I heard from my father that his Rotary Club was seeking a sister club abroad.

My father then said, 'The President Elect, Dr Shoda, is very active and internationally minded, so I'm sure he will carry it out.' He had confidence in him. He also said, 'If you could be useful to President Shoda you might be invited to join the Club.' He found two sponsors, Mr Miyazawa and Mr Ota for me to join the Club (in order to be admitted to a Rotary Club you require two sponsors). Thanks to Mr Ota and Mr Miyazawa I was admitted to the Rotary Club of Fukaya. Generally speaking, a father and his first son in Japan are in the same profession, but we were in different professions. So we were both able to belong to the same Rotary Club.

Fukaya is a long-established Rotary Club and at the time of joining, I was thirty-eight-years old – the youngest amongst its ninety members.

(3) The sister club tie-up with the Rotary Club of Changi in Singapore

Having been admitted to the Rotary Club of Fukaya, my father swiftly introduced me to the President, Dr Shoda. He gave me the impression that he was even more influential than his reputation. After he had visited several countries with his beloved wife Akiko, in seeking a sister club, he seemed to have come to the conclusion that the Rotary Club of Fukaya should have a sister club in the garden city-state of Singapore. Amongst the Rotary Clubs in Singapore he chose the Rotary Club of Changi, which is famous for its well-reputed international airport.

The executives of the Rotary Club of Fukaya had every confidence in President Shoda. His idea of having a sister club tie-up with the Rotary Club of Changi was wholeheartedly supported by the most internation-ally-minded Past Governor, Dr Fukushima, Past President Mr Hashida and almost every one in the club. They were, in one united body, preparing for a sister club tie-up with the Rotary Club of Changi to achieve the objective of Rotary International: international understanding and good-will.

In October 1988, we made our first trip to Singapore to talk about the sister club tie-up with the Rotarians of the Rotary Club of Changi. Singapore had a population of about three million people then, and amongst them 70% – 80% are of Chinese origin. There are four official languages, which are Mandarin, Malay, Tamil and English. However, there are about ten other Chinese dialects spoken in Singapore. Amongst the different Chinese dialects-speaking people, English is used as their lingua franca. Singapore is a real international city-state.

Looking back on my college days some twenty-five years ago, the first student I became friendly with was a Chinese Singaporean in the hall of residence of the University of London. That was the first time I was exposed to Singaporean English, which was rather different from the

English might have been relatively easier to understand compared with the English spoken by other nationals I would later encounter. When I come to think of it, because of my poor English in those days I would not have understood their high level of English expressions. So I had no difficulty in understanding Singaporean English, or rather it reminded me of my good Singaporean friend in the hall of residence.

So in spite of the fact that I was the only interpreter for both sides, I had the impression that the Singaporean delegates had no difficulty with my English accent and accepted me without difficulty.

However, we had some awkward moments at the first meeting with the Changi Rotarians when we were discusing the sister club tie-up of our two clubs. In our delegation, we had a couple of past presidents who fought in Singapore during the war. There must have been some Singaporean delegates who were not happy with the Japanese Imperial Army occupation during the war as well. So it is no exaggeration to say that this meeting started in a somewhat sceptical and tense atmosphere.

The delegates of both Clubs made a great effort in expelling the sceptical atmosphere. The atmosphere of the meeting was in time changed to a peaceful and trusting one where we freely exchanged our opinions. We were therefore able to agree on what should be included in the agreement of the sister club tie-up. I witnessed and learned a great deal from working as the interpreter for both sides there. I came to realize that the friendship and reliance of Rotarians was powerful enough to go beyond the national boundaries, and if they had not had the pride and consciousness as Rotarians, the first meeting would not have ended on a positive note. What I would especially like to emphasize here is the eagerness for international goodwill, and the leadership demonstrated by President Tan Leong Teck of Changi Rotary Club and President Shoda of Fukaya Rotary Club, which is typical of the Rotary spirit.

During our first goodwill visit to Singapore, there were various events, the talks between the clubs, a goodwill golf match, sightseeing and so on, thus I was rushed off my feet all the time. As I was rather inexperienced, I might not have been able to work as much as the other delegates in our group expected me to. Despite the fact that I was not able to meet their expectations in Singapore, they all thanked me for looking after them well at the home-coming party. On returning to my home after the party, when I recalled the warmth of their hearts and the splendour of the international goodwill shown, I was moved to tears. I felt extremely pleased to have become a Rotarian.

After the visit, the talks of the sister club tie-up proceeded well. The Rotary Club of Fukaya and the Rotary Club of Changi concluded the

Sister Club Tie-Up Agreement on 25 May, 1989 in the city of Fukaya, and consequently we acquired Rotarian relatives in each other's countries.

Amongst my Singaporean 'relatives', Past President Dr Gong of Changi R.C. is indeed a dedicated Rotarian and like an elder brother to me. After the Sister Club Tie-Up Agreement between Fukaya R.C. and Changi R.C., I have come to realize that international friendship can really be nurtured. Thanks to Rotary International, I am now writing this chapter of my book while on board a plane bound for Singapore. I will soon be meeting my Singaporean mentor, Charter President Tan Leong Teck, Dr Gong and all my Singaporean relatives. I feel as if I was going to see long lost friends. I am quite excited about it. This, I think, is what Rotary International is all about!

(4) The friendship club tie-up with Roissy Rotary Club of Paris

In the following year, Mr Ota became our president, and he was very vigorous and active. As we had concluded the Sister Club Tie-Up Agreement with the Rotary Club of Changi in Singapore the previous year, he was thinking of doing something international in his tenure. So I suggested that we should seek a sister club somewhere in Europe. At the time, I happened to make a business trip to Paris and London, and was asked to visit some Rotary Clubs in Paris. I had been to Paris a few times before, but it was my first visit to the city as a Rotarian.

When I was writing my dissertation at the University of London in 1979 on the OECD (the Organization for Economic Cooperation and Development), whose headquarters were situated in Paris, I visited the Organization's library to gather some material for my research. I did not have a good impression of Paris then. Or rather, as I only spoke English, they were not at all kind to me! After that, in 1983, I had an opportunity to study French at the University of Grenoble in France.

Although my stay was less than a year, I managed to obtain a proficiency certificate in French. As I was able to finish my course earlier than expected, I had a month's holiday in Paris.

This time, my visit to Paris was totally different from the previous ones. It was in August, and the season as well as the climate were just right; I felt as if I were in a film. My policy to speak only French must have been right as well. The people in Paris treated me completely differently from the time I spoke nothing but English. I realized that for foreign people who speak French, Paris was a superb place.

And this time, I visited Paris as a Rotarian. First, I visited a Rotary Club which I was put in touch with by a friend of mine. They welcomed me as

And this time, I visited Paris as a Rotarian. First, I visited a Rotary Club which I was put in touch with by a friend of mine. They welcomed me as if I were a long-standing friend of theirs, for they knew in advance that I was coming there. I was pleased, and yet surprised as I had only just become a Rotarian. However, they were not interested in having a sister club tie-up with our club.

Roissy Rotary Club of Paris was the fifth club I visited, which is based in the Charles de Gaulle Airport area. I was again warmly welcomed and kindly entertained by the Rotarians there. On top of that, they were interested in having a sister club tie-up with Fukaya Rotary Club. We talked about a sister club tie-up, the relationship between France and Japan, the status of women in our respective countries and so forth for hours at the Roissy Rotary Club. During the discussion, they suggested that as we were geographically situated on the opposite sides of the globe, it would not be easy to visit each other's clubs, and that seeking a less restrictive friendship club tie-up would be more realistic than a sister club tie-up.

I could have left Paris with this proposal for a friendship club tie-up from Roissy Rotary Club, but I decided not to, because I thought it would be a great pity not to visit the most traditionally established club in Paris. So I made my way to the revered Rotary Club, 'The Paris Rotary Club'.

(5) My thanks to Rotary for the 'moving moments'

I was once again received warmly by the Rotarians of the Paris Rotary Club. I learned that most of the members were leaders in the financial world of Paris. I was flattered that they treated me, a young Rotarian, as one of their fellows.

I had a chat with some members, and one of them said to me, 'Actually, the European representative of M. Corporation has been absent for a while. Would you ask him to come and attend the regular meeting when you see him next?' However, I never met him, so I was not able to give him the message. Though this was some time ago, I would like to take this opportunity to apologize for not having been able to give him the message.

After the meeting of the Paris Rotary Club, several members kindly asked me, 'Where are you going now? Can I give you a lift?' I accepted one of their offers to take me to the Arc de Triumph.

We slowly drove through the Bois de Boulogne, which was magical and tranquil, and was totally different from high-flown and bustling Paris. I wished that the ride could have lasted forever – the Arc de Triumph appeared in time. I thanked him a great deal and promised that I would see him again.

When I was walking along the Champs Elysees, I reflected upon various times in my life, moments like my visits to Paris when I spoke no French, and the time I was in Grenoble when I was just starting to learn French. I had considered French to be impossible to speak, 'I have no talent for learning languages, and I will never be able to speak French in my entire life,' I used to say at that time. And when I came to Paris after gaining a proficiency certificate in French ... This time, in addition to being able to speak French, I was a Rotarian, and whichever Rotary Club I visited, the Rotarians always welcomed me warmly ... Oh yes! I am a Rotarian and a member of Rotary International as well! When I exclaimed in joy, there was something warm welling up from the bottom of my heart. 'Thank you Rotary for the moving moments!' I was saying to myself.

(6) The signing ceremony of the friendship club tie-up

Returning to Japan, I swiftly reported the proposal of Roissy Rotary Club to President Ota. President Ota and Mr Sekine, Director of the International Service Committee of the Fukaya Rotary Club, were very sympathetic to international exchange and were very pleased to hear the news.

They promptly took the matter to the board of directors and to the council of the past presidents and they unanimously supported the idea of a friendship club tie-up with Roissy Rotary Club in Paris.

We started an exchange of ideas by fax and phone, discussing what should be included in the agreement. I was sent to Paris a few times by President Ota to talk to them directly to sort out the final draft.

When both clubs had their discrepancies ironed out, and the date of the Signing Ceremony was fixed in Paris, at the very last minute, President Ota had to attend another international function. So, although it was rather unusual, I was asked to attend the Signing Ceremony on his behalf.

The Signing Ceremony was named 'The Japanese Evening'. It was also a dinner party with about 200 people attending and a colourful Parisian atmosphere was indeed there. The climax of the ceremony was the signing of the agreement by both representatives and speeches by the respective representatives. I was asked to make mine first. I talked about President Ota's eagerness to engage in international exchange. Everyone applauded. President Benech of Roissy Rotary Club talked about the benefits of having a friendship club in Japan, and how it was only possible to have such a friendship thanks to Rotary International and the assembly applauded with gusto. Since the signing of the Friendship Club Tie-Up

Agreement on 8 December, 1989, with the understanding of being able to visit each other's clubs freely, it has been going on up until now.

As my profession is language education in Rotary Club, I have only been talking about the international nature of Rotary Club, however, we should not forget about the domestic Rotary service activities. Most of the Rotarians who represent his or her profession are leaders in their areas. Their contributions to society are considerable.

As a Rotarian, I am still a novice of only sixteen years' Rotary experience. I am also inexperienced, as a Rotarian, as far as international affairs are concerned. But if I may be so bold, I would like to advise my fellow Rotarians to visit a Rotary Club in a foreign country if they have not yet done a make-up abroad. It is your privilege as a member of Rotary International. Mix with Rotarians from around the world who are in your profession and exchange information. I would like you, fellow Rotarians, to experience the same moving moments as I have experienced, by studying English with the Kawata Method of Learning English Conversation.

CHAPTER 9

☐ Let's learn Japanese!

With the Kawata System of Romanized Script You will not see 'Rondon' or 'Rampu' any more. (Dialogues for Beginners)

THROUGHOUT THIS BOOK, the stress has been on learning English that is clear, well articulated and understandable to authentic English speakers. I have pointed out that the sounds that you will encounter in English are different from those in Japanese.

If you are teaching English to the Japanese, one of the best ways of doing so is by getting to know more about the Japanese language.

What we are going to do is to look at Japanese, learning it from an English perspective. As we go through these exercises you will become aware of the difficulty that the Japanese language speaker encounters in learning English. You will also become aware of what Japanese actually sounds like. Work through the following chapters, and you will realize how different these two languages are! Learn about the Japanese language so that you will become more competent to teach English to Japanese people. If you do not know Japanese that is just fine, you will quickly learn it. Give it a try!

● An introduction to Japanese

(1) Japanese is poor in sounds but rich in writing

As a spoken language, Japanese is very poor in sounds. It is said that there are three times as many sounds available in English as in Japanese. It appears that this makes Japanese an easy language to learn as far as its spoken part is concerned.

However, the difficult part, for the native English speaker, is using the correct linguistic rhythm. Disregard English rhythms. Japanese is a flat, monotonous language, and when you can speak in such a way your Japanese will sound authentic.

Japanese is written in a mixture of Chinese characters called *kanji*, and two syllabaries called *hilagana* and *katakana*, both of which were born out of *kanji*. *Kanji* are mainly used for the parts of the language which communicate meaning, while *hilagana* (which used to also be called *Onna Moji*, or Women's Script) is used for indicating the functions of words, such as particles, tense endings, etc. The more square-looking *kana*, namely *katakana*, is used in a similar way to italics in English, giving prominence to certain words. *Katakana* is particularly common in words of Western origin (*gailaigo*). As you can see, Japanese is visually a rather complex language. That is why I have said that Japanese is poor in sounds but rich in writing.

(2) The Kawata System (romanized script)

In order not to impose too much difficulty on the learner, we will not use the notoriously difficult Japanese writing systems but instead employ Romanized script. We shall use the Kawata System, which is modified from the Hepburn System. (James Curtis Hepburn (1815–1911) was an American medical doctor, missionary and linguist who lived in Japan between 1859 and 1892.)

Those of you who continue your studies of Japanese will consider it strange that words like *ringo* (apple) and *Fuji-san* (Mount Fuji) are written with the letters 'r' and 'f' respectively in your textbooks according to the Hepburn System of Romanized script, while Japanese native speakers pronounce these words as '*lingo*' and '*Huji-san*', because the sounds 'f' and 'r' (the actual sound of R as it is heard in words) do not exist in Japanese. I think that those letters should never have been used in the Hepburn System in the first place. It was an enormous blunder for Hepburn to have overlooked these simple and yet important facts. Furthermore, he totally ignored the sound of L, which does exist in Japanese. So the Kawata System greatly improves the current Hepburn System by changing those two letters 'f' and 'r' to 'h' and 'l' respectively.

For instance, to the Japanese person, '*tori*' and '*toli*' (bird) sound more or less the same, whereas they are completely different to the English ear. That is why lice and rice, light and right, law and raw, etc. sound the same to the Japanese person, and they are unable to tell them apart. I feel sorry for the foreign Japanese language-learners who are confused by this. In the Kawata System, therefore, the sounds 'f' and 'r' (the actual sound of R as it is heard in words) which do not exist in Japanese are not included so as not to create unnecessary confusion. Hence 'ra, ri, ru, re, ro, rya, ryu, ryo, and fu' in the Hepburn System have been replaced with 'la, li, lu, le, lo, lya, lyu, lyo, and hu' in the Kawata System.

The Kawata System Table of romanized script of Japanese for the basic syllable structure is shown below:

a	ka	ga	sa	za	ta	da	na	ha	pa	ba	ma	ya	la	wa	-n
i	ki	gi	shi	ji	chi	ji	ni	hi	pi	bi	mi		li		
u	ku	gu	su	zu	tsu	zu	nu	hu	pu	bu	mu	yu	lu		
e	ke	ge	se	ze	te	de	ne	he	pe	be	me		le		
o	ko	go	so	zo	to	do	no	ho	po	bo	mo	yo	lo		
	kya	gya	sha	ja	cha		nya	hya	pya	bya	mya		lya		
	kyu	gyu	shu	ju	chu		nyu	hyu	pyu	byu	myu		lyu		
	kyo	gyo	sho	jo	cho		nyo	hyo	pyo	byo	myo		lyo		

(3) Pronunciation and Syllables

Westerners often describe spoken Japanese as sounding flat or monotonous. To speak Japanese, you must imagine that there is no obvious or distinctive emphasis on any part of a word or sentence, and that all syllables are given the same length and spoken at the same speed. In Japanese, the words *Ka-wa-sa-ki* and *To-yo-ta* are pronounced flatly with no part of the words stressed or lengthened; most Westerners would say Kawa-**SAA**-ki and To-**YOO**-ta. However, when you speak Japanese it is important to become familiar with rules for long and short syllables and to follow these rules. The difference between a long and a short syllable is equivalent to adding or subtracting a letter, and it will completely change the meaning of a word.

It is not easy for Westerners to recognise the difference between the following syllable combinations and so you should be careful and practise:

(1) *Hiya*, as opposed to *hya*, etc.

Whereas *hi-ya* is a combination of two syllables pronounced consecutively, *hya* is a single syllable. Try differentiating between the following pairs:

hiyaku (a leap)   *hyaku* (a hundred)
kiyō (an appointment)   *kyō* (today)

(2) Single as opposed to double consonants.
Doubling the consonant literally means holding the consonant for the length of one syllable. Try to differentiate between these pairs:

bu-ta (a pig)	*bu-t-ta* (spanked)
ha-ko (a box)	*ha-k-kō* (fermentation)
ki-ta (north)	*ki-t-ta* (cut, verb past tense)
ka-sen (a river)	*ka-s-sen* (a battle)
ka-ki (a persimmon)	*ka-k-ki* (vigor)

(3) Single as opposed to double vowels.
A double vowel is a syllable longer. The difference between a long and a short syllable in words means a difference in their meaning. In the Romanized system that is used in this book, a macron is placed over the short vowel in order to double it. Thus, 'a', 'o', and 'u' become 'ā', 'ō', and 'ū' respectively. The double 'e' is written as 'ei', while the doubled 'i' becomes 'ii'. There are some exceptions. For instance, loan words borrowed from English and other languages make use of the macron, as in 'ē' and 'ī'. Also the Japanese word for 'yes' is written 'ē'. Try to pronounce the words below:

kashu (a singer)	*kashū* (a list of songs)
kyoshitsu (a contribution)	*kyōshitsu* (a classroom)
chosho (a book)	*chōsho* (a virtue)
shujin (a master)	*shūjin* (a prisoner)

One should also pay special attention to the syllable 'n' because its sound changes depending on the letter that follows it. If a 'b', 'p', or 'm' follows, it is pronounced as though it were an 'm'. Thus *shin-bun* becomes *shimbun; den-pō* becomes *dempō*, and *an-min* changes to *ammin*.

Japanese accent is not entirely monotonous but the rising and falling pitch of syllables is extremely subtle compared to English. Normal spoken English is dependant upon strong differences in pitch whereas Japanese is not.

(4) Verbs and Sentence Structures
(1) Verbs
In Japanese, subjects do not affect verbs. In other words, regardless of whether the subject is singular or plural, first person or second, the verbs do not change their form. So far as verb tenses are concerned, there are

only two divisions of time: past tense and non-past tense. Thus, the present and future tenses are the same in Japanese.

Japanese verbs can be classified into three groups according to the way in which they conjugate.

Group A: most 'i' ending verbs (*kiki-masu, yomi-masu, yoli-masu*).
Group B: all 'e' ending verbs (*kime-masu, nige-masu, sage-masu*) and some 'i' ending ones (*ki-masu, i-masu, kali-masu*).
Group C: the two verbs *shimasu* (to do) and *kimasu* (to come).

Masu form is the 'formal form' and is suitable for a wide range of circumstances. The part of the verb that remains when the *masu* has been taken away is called the stem.

The plain form includes the dictionary form, the *nai* form, the *ta* form, and the *nakatta* form. This form corresponds to four *masu* forms. It is used in casual conversation and is used to express obligation, experience, and so forth in formal structures. Other than the *masu* form, to make each form (the *nai* form, the *ta* form, the *nakatta* form, etc.) there are certain rules which must be used, depending on the group to which the verb belongs. In this book, we are not going to delve too deeply into grammar, and so we will not show a detailed conjugation of verbs. However, the basic verb conjugation is as follows:

GROUP A *kiki masu/ kiku* (dictionary form), to hear

	kiki masu	*masu* form affirmative
Masu form	*kiki masen*	*masu* form negative
	kiki mashita	*masu* form past affirmative
	kiki masendeshita	*masu* form past negative
	kiku	plain form affirmative (dictionary form)
Plain form	*kika nai*	plain form negative (*nai* form)
	kiita	plain form past affirmative (*ta* form)
	kikanakatta	plain form past negative (*nakatta* form)
	kiite	te form
	kikeba	conditional
	kikelu	potential
	kike	imperative
	kikō	volitional
	kikalelu	passive
	kikaselalelu	causative passive 1
	kikasalelu	causative passive 2

GROUP B *kime masu/ kimelu* (dictionary form), to decide

	kime masu	*masu* form affirmative
Masu form	kime masen	*masu* form negative
	kime mashita	*masu* form past affirmative
	kime masendeshita	*masu* form past negative
	kime lu	plain form affirmative (dictionary form)
Plain form	kime nai	plain form negative (*nai* form)
	kime ta	plain form affirmative (*ta* form)
	kime nakatta	plain form past negative (*nakatta* form)
	kimete	*te* form
	kimeleba	conditional
	kimelalelu	potential
	kimelo	imperative
	kimeyō	volitional
	kimelalelu	passive
	kimesaselu	causative
	kimesaselalelu	causative passive I

GROUP C *shi masu/ sulu* (dictionary form), to do

	shi masu	*masu* form affirmative
Masu form	shi masen	*masu* form negative
	shi mashita	*masu* form past affirmative
	shi masendeshita	*masu* form past negative
	sulu	plain form affirmative (dictionary form)
Plain form	shi nai	plain form negative (*nai* form)
	shita	plain form past affirmative (*ta* form)
	shinakatta	plain form past negative (*nakatta* form)
	shite	*te* form
	suleba	conditional
	dekilu	potential
	shilo	imperative
	shiyō	volitional
	salelu	passive
	saselu	causative
	saselalelu	causative passive I

(2) Sentence Structure
The following five patterns represent the basic Japanese sentence structure.

1. [subject] *wa/ ga* [intransitive verb].
2. [subject] *wa/ ga* [indirect object] *ni* [intransitive verb].
3. [subject] *wa/ ga* [direct object] *o* [transitive verb].
4. [subject] *wa/ ga* [indirect object] *ni* [direct object] *o* [transitive verb].
5. [place] *ni* [subject] *ga* [*alimasu / imasu*].

Whether the subject is followed by the particles 'wa' or 'ga' depends on the context. If the subject is contrasted with other things, or if only partial information about the subject is given, then 'wa' replaces 'ga'. In general, 'ga' is used when the stress is more on the subject of the sentence.

(5) Foreign Loan Words (*gailaigo*)

In Japanese, most of the *gailaigo* are written in *katakana* in order to show that they have a foreign origin. Foreign people in Japan are often confused by the *katakana* of the borrowed words as they strike the foreigner as peculiar.

As there are not such sounds as f, r, v, θ, ð in Japanese, Japanese people pronounce '*bideo*' for 'video', '*camela*' for 'camera', '*lajio*' for 'radio', etc. they change them conveniently into sounds they can pronounce and use them with the foreign people. On top of that, because of the fact that most of the *gailaigo* are still written according to the Hepburn System of Romanized script, foreign people will be even more confused with words such as '*ressun* (lesson)', '*rampu* (lamp)', '*Rondon* (London)', etc. when they find them in their textbooks for the Japanese language studies.

However when foreign people appreciate that the sounds 'f, r, v, θ' and 'ð' do not exist in Japanese, they might be well advised to pronounce these words in the manner that the Japanese do so as not to hamper communication.

Loan words are generally adapted to the Japanese syllable structure and sounds by inserting vowels between consonant clusters and after the final consonant. Thus the English 'Christmas' becomes *ku-li-su-ma-su*, 'album' *a-lu-ba-mu*, 'hot' *ho-t-to*, and 'Bill' *Bi-lu*.

(6) You will be better acquainted with Japanese and the Japanese

The author concedes that since this book was originally written in Japanese for the Japanese, even though some alterations and additions have been made to the English version, it is still not extensive enough as a Japanese textbook for Japanese language students. In particular, grammar explanations have not been dealt with in depth.

However, the author hopes that the reader will be acquainted with the national character of the Japanese and their language after reading this book. Thus, in future encounters with Japanese people, the reader will be better equipped to carry out his or her business, whatever that might be.

● Dialogues for beginners (Ten dialogues)

The dialogues that follow are conducted between the following cast of players:

John Bird: an English teacher, from England, in his mid-thirties who lives with the Kawata family.

Emi Kawata: a ten-year old Japanese girl attending a primary school in Hukaya city, Saitama Prefecture.

Ei Kawata: Emi's eight-year-old sister who attends the same school.

Jenī (Jenny), Tomomi, Yuppi, and Kanako are school friends of Emi.

In each dialogue the children use a style of Japanese that is more formal than they would probably do with their English teacher. However, by adding this level of formality you, the reader, can use and adapt these conversations when talking to adults in real-life situations.

Each dialogue comes with a translation that is free rather than literal. Because of cultural differences between the English and the Japanese, some expressions would seem strange if translated literally. Similarly, since Japanese is more vague than English, a literal translation might sound a little awkward.

Notes on some of the essential words and points of grammar follow each dialogue. You will see '~' in the notes, which means '........' , or 'blah, blah, blah (etc., etc., etc.)' in English.

You should read over each dialogue until you are familiar with the usage. If you are learning with a friend you might want to role-play.

(1) Namae wa nan to iimasu ka? – What's your name, please?

JOHN: Konnichi wa.

Ei: Konnichi wa.

JOHN   Namae wa nan to iimasu ka?

Ei: Kawata Ei desu.

JOHN: Ei wa anata no namae desu ka?

Ei: Hai, sō desu. Kawata wa, watashi no myōji desu.

JOHN: *Doko ni sunde ilu no desu ka?*
EI: *Hukaya ni sunde imasu.*
JOHN: *Hukaya no doko ni sunde imasu ka?*
EI: *Hukaya-chō ni sunde imasu.*
JOHN: *Aligatō.*
EI: *Dōitashimashite.*

JOHN: Hello.
EI: Hello.
JOHN: What's your name, please?
EI: My name is Ei Kawata.
JOHN: Is Ei your first name?
EI: Yes, it is. Kawata is my family name.
JOHN: Where do you live, please?
EI: I live in Hukaya.
JOHN: Where in Hukaya do you live?
EI: In Hukaya-cho.
JOHN: Thank you.
EI: Thank you.

(One) *wa.* 'X *wa* Y *desu*' means that 'X is Y '. Things or people in Japanese are indicated by using this pattern. The particle '*wa*' marks the subject of a sentence, whereas '*desu*' has the English meaning of 'is'. Hence X is identified by Y with '*desu*', which means 'is' in English.

(Two) *to.* This *to* is a quoting particle and indicates what has been said, similar to the English 'that'. Thus *Kanojo wa tsukalete ilu to itte masu*, means 'She says that she is tired'. Note that in English this 'that' is sometimes left out of the sentence without any loss of meaning ('She says she is tired'), whereas it must always be present in Japanese.

(Three) *nan/ nani:* 'what?' '*nan*' and '*nani*' are different ways of pronouncing the same word.

(Four) *ka.* This is the equivalent of the question mark '?' in English. This 'X *wa* Y *desu*', which means that 'X is Y ', can be turned into a question ('Is X Y?') by the addition of this question particle '*ka*': 'X *wa* Y *desu ka.*'

(Five) *no.* There are several different ways of using this word in Japanese. This '*no*' is an ownership particle, similar to the 'of ' in English. So in Japanese the word order '*anata no*' is the same as the English 'of you', that is 'yours'. *Ei wa anata no namae desu ka* – Is Ei your first name?

(Six) *desu.* This means 'am', 'are', or 'is'. Thus 'I am a teacher' – *Watashi wa kyōshi desu.* 'We are teachers' – *Watashitachi wa kyōshi desu.* 'She is a teacher' – *Kanojo wa kyōshi desu.* Note however that when translating this sentence, 'There is a pen in the box' we do not use *desu* but rather *masu*, hence *Hako no naka ni pen ga alimasu.*

(Seven) *doko ni, Hukaya ni.* Here the *'ni'* can be thought of as a location particle used after place nouns indicating where the action of the sentence takes place.

(Eight) ~ *sunde imasu.* Here the *te* form + *imasu* is used to indicate a habitual action or a state of being.

(2) *Denwa bangō wa nanban desu ka?* – What is your telephone number?

JENNY: *Kyō wa nan yōbi desu ka? Emi-san?*
EMI: *Kinyōbi desu.*
JENNY: *Sole dewa ashita denwa shimasu. Denwa bangō wa nanban na no?*
EMI: *571-5050 (gō nana ichi no gō zelo gō zelo) desu.*
JENNY: *571-5050 (gō nana ichi no gō zelo gō zelo) desu ne.*
EMI: *Sō desu. Anata no bangō wa nanban desu ka, Jenī-san?*
JENNY: *573-3547 (gō nana san no san gō yon nana) desu.*
EMI: *573-3547 (gō nana san no san gō yon nana) desu ne.*
JENNY: *Sō desu.*
EMI: *Aligatō.*
JENNY: *Dōitashimashite.*

JENNY: What day of the week is it today, Emi?
EMI: It's Friday.
JENNY: Then I'll telephone you tomorrow. What's your telephone number?
EMI: It's 571-5050.
JENNY: So, it's 571-5050.
EMI: Correct. What's yours, Jenny?
JENNY: It's 573-3547.
EMI: So, it's 573-3547.
JENNY: Right.
EMI: Thank you.
JENNY: Not at all.

(One) ~ *nan ban 'na no'.* This *'no'* is the feminine sentence ending, which is also used by men if they are asking a question of a woman with whom they are on close terms.

(Two) *denwa-sulu*: To telephone (an action noun). Many nouns of Chinese or Western origin become verbs by attaching '*sulu*' to them, as in this example.

(Three) *zelo*. In accordance with the Kawata System of Romanized script, as there is no such sound as 'R' in Japanese, we use the spelling '*zelo*' instead of 'zero'.

(Four) ~ *ne*. A sentence ending particle, which is intended to urge the agreement of the person asked. It's very much like, 'Isn't it?' in English.

(3) 'Watashi wa genki desu' to wa itsumo ienai node – People don't always say, 'I'm fine.'

JOHN: Gokigen ikaga desu ka, Yuppi-san?
YUPPI: Okage de genki desu.
JOHN: Anata wa, Jenī-san?
JENNY: Mā mā desu, aligatō.
JOHN: Emi-san, wa dō desu ka?
EMI: Watashi wa onaka ga suite imasu.
JOHN: Watashi mo desu yo. Tomomi-san, anata wa dō desu ka?
TOMOMI: Watashi wa nemuin desu.
JOHN: Sole wa taihen desu ne. Kanako-san wa dō desu ka?
KANAKO: Watashi wa tsukalete imasu.
JOHN: Sole wa yoku nai desu ne. Ei-san, anata wa dō desu ka?
EI: Okage de, watashi wa genki desu.
JOHN: Sole wa yokkata (Anshin shimashita).

JOHN: How are you, Yuppi?
YUPPI: Not bad, thank you.
JOHN: How are you, Jenny?
JENNY: So so, thank you.
JOHN: How are you, Emi?
EMI: I'm hungry.
JOHN: So am I. How are you, Tomomi?
TOMOMI: I'm sleepy.
JOHN: I'm sorry to hear that. How are you, Kanako?
KANAKO: I'm tired.
JOHN: That's too bad. How are you, Ei?
EI: I'm fine, thank you!
JOHN: Great!

(One) ~ *ienai* : ~ can't say ~. This is a plain form negative (*nai* form).

(Two) ~ *to wa itsumo ienai node:* As (subject) can not always say that-.

(Three) ~ *yo:* A sentence-ending particle, which is used to alert the listener. It's like an exclamation mark in English.

(Four) ~ *anata wa dō desu ka?:* This '*dō* ' means 'how'.

(Five) ~ *nemuin desu:* to be sleepy. Plain form + ~ *n desu:* a colloquial *masu* form.

(4) *Kazoku wa nannin desu ka? – How many people are there in your family?*

JOHN:	*Konnichi wa, Emi-san. Anata wa nannin kazoku desu ka?*
EMI:	*Go-nin desu.*
JOHN:	*Kazoku no minasan o shōkai shite kulemasen ka?*
EMI:	*Watashi ni wa o–bāchan ga ite, namae o Setsuko to iimasu.*
JOHN:	*Sono o-bāchan wa o-tō-san no o-kā-san desu ka?*
EMI:	*Hai, sō desu. Soshite, watashi no chichi wa Eiichi to iimasu.*
JOHN:	*Tsugi wa anata no o-kā-san?*
EMI:	*Sō desu. Namae wa Miyuki desu.*
JOHN:	*Shimai ka kyōdai wa imasu ka?*
EMI:	*Hai, imasu. Ei to iu namae no imōto ga imasu.*
JOHN:	*Soshite, anata jishin desu ne?*
EMI:	*Hai, sō desu.*
JOHN:	*Aligatō.*
EMI:	*Dōitashimashite.*

JOHN:	Hello, Emi. How many people are there in your family?
EMI:	We are five.
JOHN:	Who are they, please?
EMI:	I have a grandmother called Setsuko.
JOHN:	Is she your father's mother?
EMI:	Yes, she is. And my Dad is called Eiichi.
JOHN:	Your Mum comes after that?
EMI:	That's it. Her name is Miyuki.
JOHN:	Do you have any sisters or brothers?
EMI:	Yes, I do. I have a younger sister called Ei.
JOHN:	And yourself, Emi?
EMI:	Yes.
JOHN:	Thank you.
EMI:	Not at all.

(One) ~ *minasan o shōkai shite:* In this case the 'o' indicates that the noun which it follows is the object of the verb.

(Two) ~ *shite kulemasen ka?:* ~ please introduce ~. *te* form + *kulemasen ka?* This means, 'would you please do ~ ', when your request might cause some trouble or inconvenience to the party being asked.

(Three) *o-bāchan, o-tō-san, o-kā-san:* This 'o' is an honourific prefix that makes a word polite and respectful. This honourific 'o' prefix, however, should never be used about oneself. So when I ask you, *O-genki desu ka?* ('How are you?'), you should drop the 'o' on your reply and say *Genki desu* ('I'm fine'). You should not say *O-genki desu,* although this is a very common mistake that beginners make.

(Four) *'Watashi ni wa o-bāchan ga ite, ~':* A double particle '*ni wa*' means 'for, in, in order to', etc. In this case, '*ni wa*' means 'for' and is emphasising the word '*watashi*', 'I', which is the subject of the sentence: The '~ *ga ite*' means (subject) has/have ~ and ~ . It indicates possession or ownership of the subject.

(5) *Nansai desu ka? – How old are you?*

JOHN:	*Emi-san wa nansai desu ka?*
EMI:	*10 (jussai) desu.*
JOHN:	*Imōto no Ei-san wa nansai desu ka?*
EMI:	*8 (hassai) desu.*
JOHN:	*O-tō-san wa nansai desu ka?*
EMI:	*48 (yonjyū hassai) desu.*
JOHN:	*O-kā-san wa nansai desu ka?*
EMI:	*39 (sanjū kyūsai) desu.*
JOHN:	*O-bāchan wa nansai desu ka?*
EMI:	*70 (nanajyū sai) desu.*
JOHN:	*Aligatō.*
EMI:	*Dōitashimashite.*

JOHN:	How old are you, Emi?
EMI:	I'm ten.
JOHN:	How old is your sister Ei?
EMI:	She's eight.
JOHN:	How old is your father?
EMI:	He's forty-eight.
JOHN:	How old is your mother?
EMI:	She's thirty-nine.

JOHN: How old is your grandmother?
EMI: She's seventy.
JOHN: Thank you.
EMI: Not at all.

(One) *Emi-san, Ei-san, o-tō-san, o-kā-san:* These are the Japanese equivalents for Mr., Mrs., Miss, Ms., and are always attached to somebody's name, either surname or given name. They are also used when addressing one's father or mother.

(Two) *o-bāchan:* The form '-chan' is an informal and familiar way of addressing somebody and is used when talking to, or about, children or close relatives, or friends.

(6) Gakkō wa suki desu ka? – Do you like school?

JOHN: *Emi-san. Anata wa gakkō ga suki desu ka?*
EMI: *Hai, suki desu.*
JOHN: *Donna kyōka ga suki desu ka?*
EMI: *Sansū to ongaku to kokugo ga suki desu. (Shakai, Iika, taiku, zukō)*
JOHN: *Dono kyōka ga ichi-ban suki desu ka?*
EMI: *Kokugo ga ichi-ban suki desu.*
JOHN: *Hōkago wa nani o shimasu ka?*
EMI: *Getsu-yōbi wa, suimingu sukūlu ni ikimasu. Ka-yōbi wa, Eigo o benkyō-shimasu. Sui-yōbi wa, shodō no o-keiko desu. Kin-yōbi wa, piano desu. Do-yōbi wa, jūdo o shimasu.*
JOHN: *Totemo isogashii desu ne.*
EMI: *Hai.*
JOHN: *Gambatte kudasai.*
EMI: *Aligatō.*

JOHN: Do you like school, Emi?
EMI: Yes, I do.
JOHN: Which subjects do you like?
EMI: I like maths, music and Japanese. (social studies, science, physical education, arts and craft)
JOHN: Which one of these do you like best?
EMI: I like Japanese best.
JOHN: What do you do after school, Emi?
EMI: On Mondays, I have a swimming lesson. On Tuesdays, I have an English class. On Wednesdays, I have a calligraphy class. On Fridays, I have a piano lesson. On Saturdays, I have a judo class.

JOHN: You are very busy.
EMI: Yes.
JOHN: Keep it up.
EMI: Thank you.

(One) The days of the week are as follows: *Getsuyōbi* (Monday), *Kayōbi* (Tuesday), *Suiyōbi* (Wednesday), *Mokuyōbi* (Thursday), *Kinyōbi* (Friday), *Doyōbi* (Saturday), and *Nichiyōbi* (Sunday).

(Two) *Shodō no o-keiko*: A calligraphy class, or lesson. Remember that the art of writing Japanese is very important as it is considered a virtue in Japan to be able to write the language well.

(Three) *soloban kyōshitsu*: a class (lesson) in abacus. It is a virtue in Japan to be good at calculating.

(7) *Supōtsu wa suki desu ka? – Do you like sports?*

JOHN: *Emi-san, anata wa supōtsu wa suki desu ka?*
EMI: *Hai, suki desu.*
JOHN: *Donna supōtsu o shimasu ka?*
EMI: *Jūdo to tenisu o shimasu. Oyoidali mo shimasu.*
JOHN: *Dale to sulu no desu ka?*
EMI: *Tenisu wa chichi to shimasu.*
JOHN: *Jūdo wa dale to sulu no desu ka?*
EMI: *Chichi wa jūdo no kōchi desu.*
           Chichi ga watashi to imōto no Ei ni oshiete kulemasu.
JOHN: *O-tō-san to oyogimasu ka?*
EMI: *Hai, tokidoki. Demo, watashi wa shū ni ikkai suimingu skūlu ni kayotte imasu.*
JOHN: *Aligatō.*
EMI: *Dōitashimashite.*

JOHN: Do you like sports, Emi?
EMI: Yes, I do.
JOHN: What do you play?
EMI: I do judo and play tennis. I also swim.
JOHN: Whom do you play with?
EMI: I play tennis with my Dad.
JOHN: How about judo?
EMI: My Dad is a judo instructor. He teaches my sister Ei and myself.
JOHN: Do you swim with him?

EMI: Yes, sometimes. But I go to a swimming class once a week.
JOHN: Thank you.
EMI: Not at all.

(One) ~ *oyoidali mo* ~: ~ swim as well. *ta* form + *-li*. *-li shimasu,* indicating actions that are done alternatively.

(Two) *dale to sulu?:* This literally means, 'Whom do you play with?'

(Three) *chichi wa:* When describing one's father to someone outside the family, he is humbly addressed '*chichi*' instead of '*o-tō-san*'.

(Four) ~ *kayotte imasu:* ~ go to ~. The *te* form + *imasu;* this expresses the present progressive tense, a habitual action or a state of being.

(8) *Gaikoku e yukitai desu ka? – Would you like to go abroad?*

JOHN: *Gaikoku e yukitai desu ka, Emi-san?*
EMI: *Hai, yukitai desu.*
JOHN: *Doko e yukitai desu ka?*
EMI: *Shingapōlu e yukitai desu.*
JOHN: *Dō-shite desu ka?*
EMI: *Shingapōlu ni wa chichi no tomodachi ga takusan ilu no desu.*
JOHN: *Sō desu ka, chikai uchi ni ikelu to ii desu ne.*
EMI: *Sō desu ne.*
JOHN: *Aligatō.*
EMI: *Dōitashimashite.*

JOHN: Would you like to go abroad, Emi?
EMI: Yes, I would.
JOHN: Where would you like to go?
EMI: I would like to go to Singapore.
JOHN: Why?
EMI: Because my Dad has many friends there.
JOHN: I see. I hope that you'll be able to go there soon.
EMI: So do I.
JOHN: Thank you.
EMI: Not at all.

(One) ~ *yukitai desu:* Means ~ would like to go ~. Stem + *tai desu;* expresses the speaker's desire of wanting to do something.

(Two) *e:* This particle indicates a destination or direction.

(Three) ~ *ni wa* ~: A double particle meaning 'in'.

(Four) *chikai uchi ni:* Shortly.

(9) *'Bēgo' to 'Eigo' wa dō chigau no desu ka?* — What are the differences between English and American English?

EMI: *Konnichi wa, Jon-san.*
JOHN: *Konnichi wa, Emi-san.*
EMI: *Kikitai koto ga alimasu, Jon-san.*
JOHN: *Nan desu ka?*
EMI: *Bēgo to Eigo wa chigaimasu yo ne?*
JOHN: *Sole hodo dewa alimasen kedo.*
EMI: *Kihonteki-na chigai o oshiete kudasai.*
JOHN: *Ii desu yo. Eikoku-jin ga, 'hɔt <hot>, dɔg <dog>, dɔctə, <doctor>' to hatsuon-sulu toki, Amelika-jin wa onaji tango o 'hat <hot>, dag <dog>, dactər <doctor>' to hatsuon-shimasu yo ne.*
EMI: *To iu koto wa, Eikoku-jin ga 'ɔ<o>' no hatsuon o sulu toki, Amelika-jin wa sono oto o 'a <a>' to hatsuon sulu to iu koto desu ka?*
JOHN: *Sonotōli desu. Hokani tatoeba, Amelika-jin wa tango no saigo no 'R' o hatsuon-sulu kala, 'four<fɔːr>' to iu kedo, Eikoku-jin wa owali no 'R' o hatsuon-shinai de 'four<fɔː>' to iimasu.*
EMI: *To iu koto wa, Amelika-jin ga 'kaːr <car>, flaʊər <flower>, juər<your>' to iu toki, Eikoku-jin wa 'kaː <car>, flauə<flower>, juə <your>' to hatsuon sulu to iu koto desu ne.*
JOHN: *Yoku wakali mashita ne, Emi-san.*
EMI: *Aligatō, Jon-san.*
JOHN: *Dōitashimashite.*

EMI: Hello, John.
JOHN: Hello, Emi.
EMI: I have a question to ask you, John.
JOHN: Go on, Emi?
EMI: American English and English (Standard) English are different, aren't they?
JOHN: Not that much.
EMI: Would you tell me the basic differences, please?
JOHN: All right. While the English pronounce words like 'hɔt <hot>, dɔg <dog>, dɔctər <doctor>', Americans tend to pronounce them as 'hat <hot>, dɑg <dog>, dactər <doctor>'.
EMI: So when the English say 'o < ɔ >', the Americans say 'a < ɑ >?'

JOHN: That's it. Another thing is that while the Americans pronounce the letter 'R' at the end of a word, as for example in 'fɔ:r', the English tend not to pronounce the letter, saying 'fɔ:', without the final 'R'.

EMI: So, while the Americans say 'kɑ:r <car>, flauər <flower>, juər <your>', the English say 'kɑ: <car>, flauə <flower>, juə <your>'.

JOHN: Spot-on, Emi.

EMI: Thank you, John.

JOHN: My pleasure.

(One) ~ *no desu ka?:* ~ would you ~? Plain form + *no* ? is used in casual speech, *no* is used as a question marker instead of *ka*.

(Two) ~ *kedo:* End of a sentence, meaning 'though, but, although'.

(Three) *Kihonteki-na:* Basic

(10) *Ashita, ie ni oide yo – Come to my house tomorrow.*
Note that this dialogue takes place between close friends and so they use informal speech. For instance they do not call one another '-*san*'.

EI: *Hai, Kawata desu.*

JENNY: *Moshi moshi, Jenī desu ga, Mimi-san wa imasu ka?*

EI: *Chotte matte kudasai, ima kawalimasu.*

JENNY: *Aligatō.*

EMI: *Jenī¯, omatase.*

JENNY: *Ii no yo, Mimi. Ashita no koto nanda kedo.*

EMI: *Nanika alu no?*

JENMY: *O-kā-san ga gakkō ga owattala ie ni konaikatte itte lu wa.*

EMI: *Uleshii wa. Nani o sulu yotei nano?*

JENNY: *Kēki o yakō to omou no.*

EMI: *Watashi-tachi dake-de?*

JENNY: *O-kā-san mo tetsudatte kulelu wa. Shimpai shinai de.*

EMI: *Yokatta. Watashi wa hulūtsu-kēki ga tsukulitai na.*

JENNY: *Watashi mo yo.*

EMI: *Tanoshimi da wa. Denwa aligatō.*

JENNY: *Dōitashimashite. Ashita ne. Sayōnala, Mimi.*

EMI: *Sayōnala, Jenī¯.*

EI: Hello, Kawata speaking.

JENNY: Hello. This is Jenny speaking. May I speak with Mimi, please?

EI: Hang on, I'll get her for you.
JENNY: Thanks.
EMI: Sorry to keep you waiting, Jenny.
JENNY: That's all right, Mimi. It's about tomorrow.
EMI: What's going on?
JENMY: My Mum says that you can come to my place after school.
EMI: Sounds great. What are we going to do then?
JENNY: Let's bake some cakes.
EMI: On our own?
JENNY: My Mum will be helping us. Not to worry.
EMI: Good. I would like to make some fruitcakes if possible.
JENNY: So would I.
EMI: I'll look forward to that. Thanks for ringing.
JENNY: Not at all. See you tomorrow then. Goodbye, Mimi.
EMI: Goodbye, Jenny.

(One) *Hai, Kawata desu:* This is Kawata speaking... Unlike in England, generally, one does not say one's phone number in Japan when answering a telephone call.

(Two) *Jenī desu ga:* This 'ga' works as a conjunction 'and', connecting both of the clauses.

(Three) *Mimi:* That's Emi's nickname.

(Four) *o-matase:* 'Sorry to keep you waiting.' This is an informal way of saying *'0-mataseshimashita.'*

(Five) *~ nanda kedo:* 'It's about ~ .' This is an informal way of saying '~ *na no desu ga'.*

(Six) *Nani ka alu no?:* 'What's going on?' In formal speech it would end with '*no desu ka?'*

(Seven) *~ ga owattala:* 'After finishing ~,' The *ta* form + *la* gives a conditional pattern (if, when).

(Eight) *~ konaikatte itte lu wa :* '~ says that you can come to ~ .' In ordinary speech you would use the form '*kite hoshi to itte imasu'* instead of this. The *te* form + *imasu* expresses the present progressive tense, a habitual action or a state of being. The *te* form is also used as a connective to show the order in which actions occur consecutively.

(Nine) *~ na:* 'I hope that ~.'

(Ten) ~ *wa:* This '*wa*' is the feminine sentence ending and is different from the '*wa*' which comes after a noun.

(Eleven) *Shimpai shinai de:* Not to worry. A more formal way of ending the sentence would have been to use '~ *de kudasai*'.

CHAPTER 10

The months of the year – Dialogues for beginners and intermediate level

ONCE YOU HAVE PRACTISED the first series of dialogues that were contained in the previous chapter, you might want to try these. The present chapter contains twelve dialogues that are more advanced and use increasingly more difficult Japanese. You will note that your Japanese language skills are improving and hopefully you will be able to recognize a great deal of learned material in each new situation.

Master each dialogue before moving on to the next one. You should repeat a dialogue several times. As before, each dialogue is followed by a free translation and by notes that introduce cultural and seasonal events in the text.

The dialogues are between the following cast of players:

John Bird: an English teacher, from England, in his mid-thirties who lives with the Kawata family.

Eita Kawata: a thirteen-year old Japanese boy attending a junior high school in Hukaya city, Saitama Prefecture. *Emi-san* and *Ei-san* are his younger sisters.

Mrs Kawata: a qualified primary school teacher in her late thirties. She is the mother of *Eita-kun, Emi-san,* and *Ei-san* (Note that *-kun* is used among male friends rather than *-san*. The form *-kun* is also used when men address or refer to men who are their juniors. Junior members of a family are generally addressed or referred to by their given names, like *Eita-kun*).

The language usage is more formal and polite than you would normally expect between an English teacher and a thirteen-year-old boy, however, this will allow you to use these conversations in real-life situations.

Ichi-Gatsu Kala Jyūni-Gatsu Made
From January to December

- ### *Ichi-gatsu: Kita-hankyū to minami-hankyū*
  ### *January: The northern hemisphere and the southern hemisphere*

EITA: *Ichi-gatsu wa Nihon dewa ichiban samui tsuki desu ne, Jon-san?*
JOHN: *Hai, sō desu.*
EITA: *Eikoku demo sō desu ka?*
JOHN: *Hai, sō desu.*
EITA: *Nyūjī⁻lando dewa dō desu ka?*
JOHN: *Nyūjī⁻lando wa minami-hankyū ni alimasu. Desu kala, Nyūjī⁻lando de ichi-ban samui tsuki wa, hachi-gatsu da to omoimasu.*
EITA: *To iu koto wa, Nihon to Eikoku wa kita hankyū ni alu to iu koto desu ne.*
JOHN: *Sō desu.*
EITA: *Aligatō gozaimasu.*
JOHN: *Dōitashimashite.*

EITA: Is January the coldest month in Japan, John?
JOHN: Yes, it is.
EITA: Is it the coldest month in England as well?
JOHN: Yes, it is.
EITA: How about in New Zealand?
JOHN: New Zealand is in the southern hemisphere. So the coldest month in New Zealand is August, I think.
EITA: I see. So Japan and England are in the northern hemisphere.
JOHN: That's right.
EITA: Thank you.
JOHN: Not at all.

In Japan, at New Year, everyone has about a week off, which would traditionally be spent at home, visiting relatives, visiting the senior members of one's work, and visiting a Shinto shrine or a Buddhist temple. The winter in Japan (which stretches from about December to February), is short and mild in the southern parts of the country but becomes progressively longer and colder as you move northwards.

● Ni-gatsu: Ulūdoshi wa sekaikyōtsū
February: Leap year is a worldwide practice

JOHN: *Kotoshi no ni-gatsu wa nan nichi alimasu ka, Eita-kun?*
EITA: *28 (nijū hachi) nichi da to omoimasu.*
JOHN: *Sō desu ne.*
Demo, ni-gatsu wa itsumo 28 (nijū hachi) nichi desu ka?
EITA: *Chigaimasu. 4 (yo) nen ni ikkai ulūdoshi ga alimasu.*
JOHN: *Konomae no ulūdoshi wa itsu deshita ka? Oboete imasu ka?*
EITA: *Kyonen datta to omoimasu.*
JOHN: *Sō deshita ne.*
EITA: *Eikoku nimo ulūdoshi wa alimasu ka?*
JOHN: *Hai. Sekaikyōtsū desu.*
EITA: *Aligatō.*
JOHN: *Dōitashimashite.*

JOHN: How many days are there in February this year, Eita?
EITA: 28 days, I think.
JOHN: That's right.
But, are there always 28 days in the month of February?
EITA: No. There's a leap year every four years.
JOHN: When was the last leap year? Remember?
EITA: I think that it was last year.
JOHN: Good!
EITA: Do they have a leap year in Britain?
JOHN: Yes, they do. It's a worldwide practice.
EITA: Thank you.
JOHN: Don't mention it.

Setsubun no hi is the day that marks the transition from one season to another. Originally, there were four '*Setsubun no hi*', one for each season, however today only the one in February is celebrated by the Japanese. It is the day before the first day (*Lisshun*) of spring: according to the solar calendar either the 3rd or 4th of February. At that time, the Bean Scattering Ceremony takes place. In each Japanese household, the head of the family throws beans from the house shouting '*Huku wa uchi – oni wa soto*': Come happiness – go away demons.

● San-gatsu: Halu yo koi
March: Spring is coming

EITA:	*Kyō wa atatakai desu ne, Jon-san?*
JOHN:	*Ē, mō halu desu ne, Eita-kun.*
EITA:	*Ume ga mankai desu.*
JOHN:	*Kilei desu ne.*
EITA:	*Hai, nioi mo ii desu ne.*
JOHN:	*Minna atalashiku umale kawalō to shite ilu no desu ne.*
EITA:	*Ano oka no ue made kyōsō shimashō yo.*
JOHN:	*Ii desu yo. Yōi don. . .*
EITA:	*Mō dame desu, hashilemasen. Hayai desu ne, Jon-san wa!*
JOHN:	*Mainichi konohen o hashitte ilu kala. Totemo nalete ilu no desu yo. Sole dewa kaeli mashō ka?*
EITA:	*Hai, sō shimashō.*

EITA:	It's warm today, John.
JOHN:	Yes, spring is coming, Eita.
EITA:	The plum blossoms are in full bloom.
JOHN:	They are beautiful, aren't they?
EITA:	Yes, they are. They smell nice as well.
JOHN:	Everything is coming to life again.
EITA:	Let's run to the top of the hill, John.
JOHN:	All right. Ready... go!
EITA:	Gosh, I can't run any more. You're fast John!
JOHN:	I jog around here everyday. I'm quite used to it. Let's go home, shall we?
EITA:	Yes, let's.

The spring in Japan is from March to May. It becomes warmer gradually and everything comes to life again. The financial and academic years in Japan end in March.

● *Shi-gatsu: O-hanami ni yukimashō ka?*
  April: Shall we go and view the cherry blossoms?

JOHN:	*O-hanami ni yukimashō ka, Eita-kun?*
EITA:	*Ii desu ne, yukimashō, Jon-san.*
JOHN:	*Doko ni yukimashō ka?*
EITA:	*Kalasawadote ni sotte alukimashō yo. Kalasawa no sakula ga Hukaya dewa ichi-ban desu kala ne.*
JOHN:	*Sō desu ne. Sakula wa Nihon no kokka desu ka?*
EITA:	*Ē sō desu. Eikoku nimo kokka ga alu no desu ka?*
JOHN:	*Hai, alimasu. Bala no hana ga Igilis no kokka desu.*
EITA:	*Donna bala desu ka?*
JOHN:	*Akai bala datta to omoimasu.*

JOHN:	Shall we go and view the cherry blossoms, Eita?
EITA:	Yes, let's do that John.
JOHN:	Where shall we go?
EITA:	Let's walk along the banks of the Kalasawa River. The cherry blossoms there are the best in Hukaya.
JOHN:	Great. The cherry blossom is the national flower of Japan, isn't it?
EITA:	Yes, it is. Do you have a national flower in England?
JOHN:	Yes, we do. The rose is our national flower.
EITA:	Any particular colour?
JOHN:	I think that it's the red one.

In the month of April, the cherry blossoms are in full bloom. This month also marks the beginning of the academic and the financial years. School-leavers and those who graduate from university begin their work at this time.

● *Go-gatsu: Pikunikku ni ikitai na*
  May: I would like to go for a picnic

EITA:	*Pikunikku ni ikitai na, Jon-san.*
JOHN:	*Jitensha de dalō, Eita-kun?*
EITA:	*Sono tōli desu.*
JOHN:	*O-kā-san (Kawata-hujin) ni o-hilu no o-nigili o tsukutte molaō yo.*
EITA:	*Sō shimashō.*
JOHN:	*Sengen-yama ni jitensha de ikō yo, Eita-kun.*

EITA: *Ii desu yo. Demo, Jon-san ni wa chotto chikasugimasen ka?*
JOHN: *Shimpai nai yo. Boku wa hashitte iku koto ni shita kala ne.*
EITA: *Sole wa ii kangae desu ne.*
JOHN: *Yoshi, dekake yō.*
EITA: *Hai. Demo, mazu o-hilu o tsukutte molawanai to ne.*
JOHN: *Wasulete nai ne.*
EITA: *Mochilon desu.*

EITA: I would like to go for a picnic, John.
JOHN: On a bicycle, right, Eita?
EITA: That's what I had in mind.
JOHN: I'll ask your Mum (Mrs Kawata) to make some rice balls for lunch.
EITA: Sounds great.
JOHN: We can cycle to Mt. Sengen if you like, Eita.
EITA: All right. But isn't it too close for you, John?
JOHN: Not to worry. I've decided to jog there.
EITA: That's a good idea.
JOHN: Let's get ready.
EITA: Yes. But we have to get our lunch made first.
JOHN: You haven't forgotten it.
EITA: Of course not.

The climate in May and October is at its best in Japan. There is also a national holiday called Golden Week at the beginning of May. Golden Week begins with Greenery Day (29 April), followed by three other public holidays: Constitution Day (3 May), National Relaxation Day (4 May), and Children's Day (5 May). During the period between 29 April and 3 May, most employers grant a week's holiday.

● *Loku-gatsu: Tsuyu*
June: Rainy Season

JOHN: *Loku-gatsu ga kulu to, donna koto o omoimasu ka, Eita-kun?*
EITA: *Tsuyu (Baiu) desu ka, Jon-san.*
JOHN: *Watashi mo onaji koto ga ukande kimasu.*
EITA: *Boku wa ame no hi wa kilai desu.*
JOHN: *Watashi mo desu. Demo, ame wa sakumotsu ga sodatsu tame ni hitsuyō na no desu.*

EITA:	*Sole dewa, moshi ame ga hulana keleba, tabelumono ga nanimo nakunatte shimau no desu ne.*
JOHN:	*Sō desu.*
EITA:	*Moshi tabemono ga nani mo nakunalu to dōnalu no desu ka?*
JOHN:	*Kaigai kala shokulyō o yunyū shinakeleba nalanai deshō ne.*
EITA:	*Wakalimashita. Dakala Nihon ni wa 'tsuyu' ga hitsuyō nano desu ne.*
JOHN:	*Sono tōli desu.*

JOHN:	When June comes what do you think of, Eita?
EITA:	A rainy season, John?
JOHN:	The same thing comes to my mind.
EITA:	I don't like rainy days.
JOHN:	Nor do I. But the rain is necessary for the crops to grow.
EITA:	I see. So, if it doesn't rain, then we have nothing to eat.
JOHN:	That's it.
EITA:	If we have nothing to eat what will happen?
JOHN:	We will have to import foodstuffs from abroad.
EITA:	I see. That's why we need a rainy season in Japan.
JOHN:	Exactly.

The rainy season ('*tsuyu*') begins in June and normally lasts for about one month, although the actual period varies from year to year. In the Kanto Area, which includes Tokyo, *tsuyu* often lasts until the end of July.

● *Shichi-gatsu: Tanabata*
  July: The Festival of Stars

JOHN:	*'Tanabata' tte nan desu ka?*
MRS KAWATA:	*Hului Chūgoku no itsuwa kala kite ilu no desu. Mukashi, 'olihime' to yobalelu josei no hoshi to, 'hikoboshi' to iu dansei no hoshi ga atte, tagaini totemo aishi atte ita no desu.*
JOHN:	*Tsuzukete kudasai.*
MRS KAWATA:	*Kalela wa itsumo isshoni ita no desu.*
JOHN:	*Aishi atte ita no desu kala, betsuni mezulashii koto dewa nai to omoi masu kedo.*
MRS KAWATA:	*Sō desu ne. Desu ga, hutali wa jibuntachi no ataelaleta shigoto o shinakatta no desu. Solede Kami-sama ga okotta no desu.*

JOHN:	*Kalela wa dō natta no desu ka?*
MRS KAWATA:	*Kami-sama wa kalela o hanashite shimatta no desu. Sōshite, ichinen ni ichido, shichi-gatsu nanoka no ichi-nichi dake au koto o yulushita no desu.*
JOHN:	*To iu to, ichinen ni ichido dake shika aenaku natte shimatta to iu koto desu ka?*
MRS KAWATA:	*Sono tōli desu. Soshite sono hi ni wa, hutali no tame ni chijyō dewa omatsuli o sulu yōni natta no desu.*
JOHN:	*Sō iu koto desu ka. Tokolode, take ni bulasagatte ilu takusan no shikakui kami wa dō-iu koto desu ka? Nanika kaite alu mitai desu kedo?*
MRS KAWATA:	*Hai. Minna jibun-tachi no negai o kaku no desu.*
JOHN:	*Sō deshita ka. Yōyaku wakalimashita. Dōmo aligatō.*
MRS KAWATA:	*Dōitashimashite.*

JOHN:	What is 'Tanabata,' Mrs Kawata?
MRS KAWATA:	It comes from an old Chinese fable. Once upon a time, there was a female star called 'Olihime,' and a male star called 'Hiko-boshi' and they loved one another very much.
JOHN:	I see.
MRS KAWATA:	They were always together.
JOHN:	Nothing unusual if they were in love with one another.
MRS KAWATA:	Right. However, they didn't do the work they were assigned and so they got on the nerves of the god.
JOHN:	What happened to them?
MRS KAWATA:	The god decided to keep them apart and only allowed them to meet once a year, on the seventh of July.
JOHN:	So they could only meet once a year?
MRS KAWATA:	That's it. We have a festival to celebrate their reunion on that day.
JOHN:	I see. How about all those square-shaped pieces of plastic hanging on the bamboo? You write something on them, don't you?
MRS KAWATA:	Yes. People write their wishes on them.
JOHN:	Now I've got it. Thank you.
MRS KAWATA:	Not at all.

Tanabata (on 7 July) is a romantic festival in which one looks out for *Olihime* (a female star) and *Hikoboshi* (a male star) in the sky. However, it is right in the middle of *tsuyu* in most parts of Japan, when it is difficult to see the stars at night. It always rains because *Olihime* and *Hikoboshi* might be crying with joy at being united on that day once a year.

● *Hachi-gatsu: Natsu-yasumi* August: Summer Holidays

JOHN:	*Iyo iyo natsu-yasumi ga hajimalimashita ne, Eita-kun.*
EITA:	*Hai, Jon-san.*
JOHN:	*Natsu-yasumi no keikaku o shikkali to tatenai to sugu ni owatte shimaimasu yo.*
EITA:	*Wakalimashita, Jon-san.*
JOHN:	*Yasumi no aida wa nanji ni okimasu ka?*
EITA:	*8 (hachi) ji desu.*
JOHN:	*Motto hayaku okita hōgā ii desu. 7:30 (shichiji sanjyuppun) ni shitala dō desu ka?*
EITA:	*Wakalimashita, Jon-san. Boku wa asa no uchini benkyō-shiyōto omotte imasu.*
JOHN:	*Ii koto desu ne. Mainichi 8:30 (hachiji sanjuppun) kala 10:30 (jūji sanjuppun) made benkyō-suleba natsu-yasumi no shukudai wa suguni owalimasu yo.*
EITA:	*Solejā gambalimasu.*
JOHN:	*Shikkali yatte kudasai.*

JOHN:	At last, the summer holidays have started, Eita.
EITA:	Yes, John.
JOHN:	You know it will be over in a blink, unless you plan things well.
EITA:	I know, John.
JOHN:	What time do you get up during the holidays?
EITA:	8 a.m.
JOHN:	You had better get up earlier, Eita. How about 7:30?
EITA:	All right, John. I am thinking about studying in the morning.
JOHN:	Good, Eita. If you work from 8:30 to 10:30 every morning, then you will be able to finish your summer homework pretty soon.
EITA:	I hope so.
JOHN:	You will.

Immediately after *tsuyu*, the Japanese summer ('*natsu*') begins in earnest. It is hot and humid, and is often described as '*mushiatsui*', muggy. Everyone complains about the Japanese summer, which lasts until early September.

● *Ku-gatsu: Undōkai*
September: School Athletic Meeting

JOHN: *Ku-gatsu ni undōkai ga alunodesu ka, Eita-kun?*
EITA: *Sō desu, Jon-san. Kotoshi wa tanoshimi ni shiteimasu.*
JOHN: *Sō desu ka? Eita-kun wa hashilu no ga kilaida to omotte imashita.*
EITA: *Kilaideshita. Demo, ikkagetsu mae kala ichi-nichi 30 (sanju) kkai no hukkin o hajimete kala, konogolo mae yoli hayaku hashilelu yōni natta kigashimasu.*
JOHN: *Elai ne, Eita-kun. Gambatte kudasai.*
EITA: *Gambalimasu.*

JOHN: You have a school athletics meeting in September, don't you, Eita?
EITA: Yes, I'm looking forward to it this time.
JOHN: Is that so? I thought you didn't like running?
EITA: I used to hate it. But ever since last month, I started to do 30 sit-ups every day, I think that I'm running faster these days.
JOHN: Very good, Eita. Keep it up.
EITA: I will.

Autumn ('*aki*') begins in September and is preluded by another short rainy season with the occasional typhoon. Nowadays, towards the end of September, school athletics days are held when the climate becomes more dependable.

● *Jū-gatsu: Ensoku*
October: Excursion

JOHN: *Ashita wa ensoku desu ka, Eita-kun?*
EITA: *Hai, sō desu, Jon-san.*
JOHN: *Dokoni iku no desu ka?*
EITA: *Kodomo-Shizen-Dōbutsu-Kōen ni ikimasu.*
JOHN: *Sole wa ii desu ne. Mae ni itta koto ga aludeshō, Eita-kun?*
EITA: *Hai, alimasu. Boku wa asoko ga totemo suki desu.*
JOHN: *Donna dōbutsu ga suki desu ka, Eita-kun?*
EITA: *Koala to kangalū ga suki desu.*
JOHN: *Watashi mo suki desu. Ashita wa kitto o-kā-san (Kawata-hujin) ga oishii obentō o tsukutte kulemasu yo.*
EITA: *Yatta ne. Machidōshii na.*

JOHN: *Sole dewa hayaku yasunda hōga ii desu yo.*
EITA: *Solejyā mō neyō, o-yasumi Jon-san.*
JOHN: *O-yasumi, Eita-kun.*

JOHN: Do you have an excursion tomorrow, Eita?
EITA: Yes, I do.
JOHN: Where are you going?
EITA: We are going to 'Kodomo Shizen Doubutsu Kouen' (The Natural Animal Park for Children).
JOHN: That's nice. You have been there before, haven't you Eita?
EITA: Yes, I have. I like it very much.
JOHN: What do you like about it, Eita?
EITA: I like the koalas and the kangaroos.
JOHN: I like them too. Your Mum (Mrs Kawata) will get you a nice lunch tomorrow.
EITA: Great. I can't wait until tomorrow.
JOHN: Then you'd better have an early night, Eita.
EITA: I'll go to bed then. Good night, John.
JOHN: Good night, Eita.

The climate in October is generally stable. Japan has a special sports day on 10 October called 'Taiku No Hi ' (Physical Education Day), which commemorates the opening of the Tokyo Olympics in 1964. Throughout the country, many sports events take place around this date. Because the weather is nice and crisp, many schools also organize excursions in this month.

● Jūichi-gatsu: Onsen ni ikitai
   ## November: I would like to go to a hot spring

JOHN: *Eita-kun, shūmatsu ni onsen ni iki (yuki) masen ka?*
EITA: *Doko e iku (yuku) tsumoli desu ka, Jon-san?*
JOHN: *Gunma-ken no Takalagawa-onsen ni ikōto omotte imasu.*
EITA: *Sokotte, ippai loten-bulo no alu tokolo desu ka?*
JOHN: *Sō desu.*
EITA: *Asokotte, Nihon de ichi-ban ōkina loten-bulo desu yo ne?*
JOHN: *Osolaku ne.*
EITA: *Asoko wa oyogelu kala suki desu. Sole ni, Minakami-onsen kala mo tōku nai desu yo ne?*
JOHN: *Sō desu ne.*

EITA: *Kono jiki wa, 'Kōyō' mo kilei deshō ne.*
JOHN: *Jitsu wa, sole mo mitai no desu.*
EITA: *Tanoshimi desu.*
JOHN: *Watashi mo desu.*

JOHN: Shall we go to a hot spring this weekend, Eita?
EITA: Where do you have in mind, John?
JOHN: I would like to go to the Takalagawa Hot Spring in Gunma
           Prefecture.
EITA: Is that where they have many open-air baths?
JOHN: That's the place.
EITA: They say that it's the biggest of its kind in Japan, don't they?
JOHN: Yes, most likely.
EITA: I like it because I can swim in the baths. And it's not far from
           the Minakami Hot Spring, is it, John?
JOHN: No, it isn't.
EITA: At this time of year, we can also enjoy *Kōyō* (the leaves turning
           red) there as well.
JOHN: That's the idea, actually.
EITA: I'll look forward to that.
JOHN: So will I.

In autumn, the leaves on the trees turn spectacular colours, this is known
as 'kōyō ' (the leaves turning red). It sweeps through the country from
north to south. The Japanese are very fond of going out to the mountains
to see *kōyō*. While they are about it, they enjoy visiting hot springs as well.

● *Jūni-gatsu: Kulisumasu tte nan desu ka?*
   December: What is Christmas?

EITA: *Jon-san, 'Kulisumasu' tte dō-iu koto desu ka?*
JOHN: *Ii shitsumon desu ne, Eita-kun. Kangaeta koto mo nakatta desu.*
           'Kilisuto-sama no misa' to iu koto dakala, Kilisuto-sama no tame ni
           atsumatte o-inoli-sulu koto da to omoimasu yo.
EITA: *Sō desu ka. Kilisuto-sama wa Jūni-gatsu nijū-go nichi ni o-umale ni*
           natta no desu ka?
JOHN: *Sō da to omoimasu.*
EITA: *Dakala, sono hi ni Kilisuto-sama no o-tanjyōbi o o-iwai sulu to iu*
           koto desu ka?
JOHN: *Sono tōli desu.*

EITA: *Kangaete milu to okashii desu ne, datte Nihonjin wa hotondo Kilisuto-kyō shinja dewa nai no ni, Kilisuto-sama no o-tanjyōbi wa o-iwai sulu no desu kala ne.*

JOHN: *Eita-kun, sole dewa iya desu ka?*

EITA: *Sonna koto wa alimasen. Boku wa Kulisumas-kēki ga tabelaleleba ii no desu.*

JOHN: *Jitsuwa, watashi mo sō nano desu.*

EITA: What is 'Christmas', John?

JOHN: That's a good question, Eita. I have never thought about it. It's 'Christ + Mass', so it's a get together for Christ, I think.

EITA: I see. Was Jesus Christ born on the 25th of December?

JOHN: Yes, I believe he was.

EITA: So, isn't it the day we celebrate his birthday?

JOHN: I think that you are right.

EITA: In a way it's strange, because we are not Christians and yet we celebrate his birth.

JOHN: Don't you like it, Eita?

EITA: It's all right as long as I can have my Christmas cake.

JOHN: Me too, actually.

The Japanese celebrate New Year rather than Christmas. The reason for this is fairly obvious: there are not very many Christians in Japan. However, the Japanese like festivals and so, under the pretext of Christmas, they will get together to eat and drink. If you ask about their religious affiliation, many Japanese would tell you that they are non-practising Buddhists; they go to a temple only when there is a funeral or some such memorial service.

CHAPTER 11

☐ Situational dialogues for intermediate and advanced level

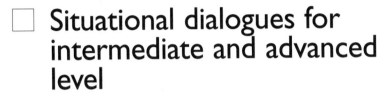

Nihon de Eigo wa manabelu no ka?
Can one learn English in Japan?

IN THIS SECTION, you will find six situational dialogues suitable for those with intermediate or advanced Japanese language skills. In the notes which accompany each dialogue, you will learn various verb-related patterns and ways of saying things. You will also learn how the author came to appreciate the differences between English and Japanese, an appreciation that led him to formulate the Kawata Method.

● *Hajimete no mensetsu: Meeting someone for the first time*

BIRD:	*Hajimemashite.*
KAWATA:	*Hajimemashite.*
BIRD:	*O-kake kudasai.*
KAWATA:	*Aligatō gozaimasu.*
BIRD:	*O-namae wa?*
KAWATA:	*Kawata Yoshikata to mōshimasu.*
BIRD:	*Dono-yō ni kaku no desu ka?*
KAWATA:	*Watashi no namae wa Y-O-S-H-I-K-A-T-A to kakimasu.*

BIRD: *Myōji wa dono-yō ni kaku no desu ka?*
KAWATA: *K-A-W-A-T-A to kakimasu*
BIRD: *'Yoshikata Kawata.' Tadashiku hatsuon-dekite imasu ka?*
KAWATA: *Zannen desu ga, sō dewa alimasen. Taila ni hatsuon-shite mite kudasai.*
BIRD: *Wakalimashita. 'Yoshikata Kawata. Yoshikata Kawata.' Iyā, dōmo seikaku ni wa hatsuon-dekinai mitai desu ne.*
KAWATA: *Kekkō desu. 'Yoshi' to yonde kudasai. Watashi no nikkunēmu desu kala.*
BIRD: *Wakalimashita. Yoshi-san, doko ni o-sumai desu ka?*
KAWATA: *Hukaya-shi to iu tokolo ni sunde imasu. Saitama-ken ni alimasu.*
BIRD: *Sō desu ka. Kumagaya mo Saitama-ken ni alimasu yo ne. Kumagaya ni wa ichido itta koto ga alimasu. Kumagaya kala wa tōi no desu ka?*
KAWATA: *Iie. Jitsu wa, Hukaya wa Kumagaya no tonali na no desu.*
BIRD: *Sō desu ka. Saigo ni nalimasu ga, denwa-bangō o o-shiete kudasai.*
KAWATA: *Hai. Zelo yon hachi gō no nana san no ichi ni san zelo (0485-73-1230) desu.*
BIRD: *Sō sulu to, zelo yon hachi gō no nana san no ichi ni san zelo (0485-73-1230) to iu koto desu ne.*
KAWATA: *Sono tōli desu.*
BIRD: *Aligatō gozaimashita.*
KAWATA: *Dōitashimashite.*

BIRD: How do you do?
KAWATA: How do you do?
BIRD: Be seated, please.
KAWATA: Thank you.
BIRD: May I have your name, please?
KAWATA: My name is Yoshikata Kawata.
BIRD: How do you spell your name, please?
KAWATA: My first name is spelt Y-O-S-H-I-K-A-T-A.
BIRD: How about your second name?
KAWATA: It's spelt K-A-W-A-T-A.
BIRD: 'Yoshikata Kawata.' Am I pronouncing your name properly?
KAWATA: No, I'm afraid not. You have to pronounce it flatly.
BIRD: I see. 'Yoshikata Kawata. Yoshikata Kawata.' No, I don't think I can pronounce your name correctly.
KAWATA: That's all right. Just call me 'Yoshi', it's my nickname.
BIRD: Good. Yoshi, where do you live?

KAWATA:	I live in a city called Hukaya. It's in Saitama Prefecture.
BIRD:	I see. I think that Kumagaya is also in Saitama. I've been to Kumagaya once. Is your place far from Kumagaya?
KAWATA:	No, it isn't. Actually, Hukaya is next to Kumagaya.
BIRD:	Is that so? Finally, may I have your telephone number, please?
KAWATA:	Certainly. It's 048-573-1230.
BIRD:	So, it's 048-573-1230.
KAWATA:	That's right.
BIRD:	Thank you.
KAWATA:	Not at all.

(One) *O-kake kudasai:* Please sit down. *o+stem+kudasai.* This is the honorific form and is designed to show respect.

(Two) ~ *mōshimasu:* This is the humble form for *iu* (to say).

(Three) ~ *shite mite kudasai:* Please try to do ~. This is the *te* form + *kudasai;* the *te* form is used often as a connective.

(Four) ~ *to yonde kudasai:* Please call me ~ , *te* form + *kudasai*.

(Five) ~ *itta koto ga alimasu:* ~ have been ~ . The *ta* form + *koto ga alimasu:* to have done something.

● *Hōmu Sutē 1: Home Stay 1*

YOSHI:	*Haitte yoloshii desu ka?*
SECRETARY:	*Dōzo.*
YOSHI:	*Konnichi wa.*
SECRETARY:	*Gokigen ikaga desu ka?*
YOSHI:	*Ē, jitsu wa, chotto.*
SECRETARY:	*Dōshita no desu ka?*
YOSHI:	*Hōmu sutē saki no koto de chotto. Dekimashitala chigau o-taku ni utsulasete itadakitai no desu ga.*
SECRETARY:	*Dō-shite desu ka?*
YOSHI:	*Dō ittala yoi no deshō ka? Watashi no tokolo no oku-sama wa go-shujin to umaku itte nai yō na no desu.*
SECRETARY:	*Anata ni wa kankei nai koto deshō. Tanin no ie no koto o sensaku sulu nowa yameta hōga ii to omoimasu yo.*
YOSHI:	*Watashi no seikatsu ni kakawatte kite ilu no de sō-iu wake ni wa ikanai no desu yo.*

SECRETARY: *Dō-iu koto desu ka?*
YOSHI: *Gakkō no panhuletto no naka ni wa, Eikoku no katei ni hōmu sutē sulu gakusei wa, sono ie no kazoku no ichi-in to shite atsukawalelu to alimasu yo ne.*
SECRETARY: *Ē. Sono tōli desu.*
YOSHI: *Shikashi, watashi wa asoko no katei dewa tadano geshukunin atsukai na no desu yo.*
SECRETARY: *Yoku wakalanai node setsumei shite itadakemasen ka?*
YOSHI: *Go-zonji no yōni ima no katei ni o-sewa ni natte kala loku shūkan tatta wake desu ga, kole made ichido no kikai o nozoite, gohun ijō no kaiwa o shita koto ga nai no desu. Ichido no kikai to iu no wa, sono ie ni tsuita saisho no hi, oku-sama to go-shujin ni pulezento o sashiageta toki no koto desu. Sole ilai, go-shujin o milu koto wa, shūmatsu igai, to itte mo kanalazu shūmatsu ni modolu wake dewa nai no desu ga, hotondo nai no desu.*
SECRETARY: *Shilimasendeshita.*
YOSHI: *Desu kala, o-kusama dake ga watashi no yui-itsu no hanashi aite na no desu. Hōmu sutē o elanda no wa mochilon Eigo no lenshū o sulu tame desu kala ne.*
SECRETARY: *Mochilon desu. Anata no o-sshalu koto wa yoku wakali-mashita. Kochila de dekilu koto wa yatte mimashō. Sole de yoloshii deshō ka?*
YOSHI: *Yoloshiku onegaishimasu.*

YOSHI: May I come in?
SECRETARY: Yes, please.
YOSHI: Hello.
SECRETARY: How are you?
YOSHI: I'm not that well, I'm afraid.
SECRETARY: What's wrong?
YOSHI: It's actually about my English family. I'm wondering if I could change to another family.
SECRETARY: You've got to tell me why.
YOSHI: Well, how shall I put it? It seems to me that the wife of my English family is not happily married.
SECRETARY: That's none of your business. You had better keep your nose out of her business.
YOSHI: It is my business when it affects my well-being.
SECRETARY: What do you mean by that?
YOSHI: If I may refer you to the school brochure, it is clearly

stipulated that a foreign student will be treated as a family member of the host family. Right?

SECRETARY: Yes, that's correct.

YOSHI: But, I'm just a lodger there.

SECRETARY: I don't understand. Would you explain it to me, please?

YOSHI: I have been with my English family for the past six weeks, as you know. Never have I had a chat longer than five minutes with the wife, except for one occasion when, on the day I arrived, I gave her and her husband presents. Since then, to start with, I hardly see the husband at home other than at the weekend, and not even every weekend.

SECRETARY: I never knew.

YOSHI: So, she is the only person around with whom I can speak. I have opted for this home stay so that I will be able to practise my English with them.

SECRETARY: Certainly. You've made your point clear. Let me see what I can do about it. Right?

YOSHI: Thank you.

(One) *Dekimashita-la* ~: If possible, conditional. It is a more polite form of 'dekile-ba'.

(Two) ~ *ittala ii no deshō ka?*: ~ shall I say? *ta* form + *la ii desu ka?* : asking for someone's advise or a suggestion.

(Three) ~ *yameta hō ga ii* ~: ~ had better stop. *ta/nai* form + *hō ga ii* ; giving advice or a suggestion (you) should do something, (you) had better do something.

(Four) ~ *atsukawalelu*: To be treated as ~; a passive form, *-lelu*.

(Five) ~ *natte kala*: After becoming ~. *te* form + *kala*; after, since, and then.

(Six) *Shilimasendeshita*: (I) didn't know, *masu* form past negative.

(Seven) ~ *sulu tame*: For doing ~. Dictionary form + *tame*; for the purpose of doing something, in order to do something.

(Eight) ~ *yatte mimashō*: I will try ~. *te* form + *mimasu;* try to do something, to do something and see how it goes or what will happen.

● *Hōmu Sutē 2: Home Stay 2*

Yoshi ga yolu osuku heya de benkyō-shite ilu to, totsuzen, nokku mo nashi ni soko no ie no onna-shujin ga doa o oshiake, kale no heya ni haitte kulu.

YOSHI: *Wa! Nani ka atta no desu ka?*
LANDLADY: *Nei, anta! Uchi wa, kono jikan ni anata ga tsukau denkidai wa gakkō kala itadaite inai no yo. Denkidai wa tottemo takai no yo, Eikoku wa.*
YOSHI: *Sō desu ka. Watashi no gakkō to otaku no aida de donna keiyaku ga kawasaleta ka zonjimasen ga, tōzen koko dewa suki na dake benkyō-sasete itadakelu to omotteimashita.*
LANDLADY: *Walui kedo, sole wa ninshiki busoku ne. Sole ni, gakkō ni benkyō-beya ga alu deshō. Dō-shite soko o tsukawanai no?*
YOSHI: *Tsukatte imasu. Demo gogo kuji ni wa shimatte shimauno desu.*
LANDLADY: *Sonna ni benkyō-shitelunala o-tsukale deshō. Koko ni kaettala yasumu beki yo.*
YOSHI: *Watashi wa yasumi ni Eikoku ni kita no dewa nai no desu yo. Nihon no daigaku o ichi-nen kyūgaku shite kite ilu no desu. Kuni dewa, tomodachi wa tottemo gambatte ilu hazu desu. Kalela ni wa maketaku nai no desu. Ichi-byō datte mudani shitaku nai no desu yo.*
LANDLADY: *Demo denki wa tsukawaselalenai wa yo. Tottemo takai no yo. Laito o kesu wa yo.*
YOSHI: *Nani o sulu no desu ka? Chō mukatsuku na! Watashi wa otaku no isōlō desu ka? Gakkō no panhuletto ni yolu to, gaikoku no gakusei wa Eikoku no katei de ichiō o-kyaku to shite atsukatte itadakelu to alimashita yo ne. Mattaku shingai da na.*
LANDLADY: *Watashi mo yo.*
YOSHI: *Wakalimashita. Sole dewa, dakyō-an o dashimashō. Watashi wa izuleni shite mo benkyō-shinakeleba nalanai wake desu kala, gakkō de talinai bun wa watashi ga anata ni chokusetsu o-shihalai shimasu. Sole de dō desu ka?*
LANDLADY: *Sō shite itadakeleba kekkō da to omoimasu yo.*

Late at night, when Yoshi is studying in his room, all of a sudden, without a knock, the door swings open and the landlady rushes into his room.

YOSHI: Gosh! What's going on?
LANDLADY: Look! Your school is not paying for the electricity that you

are using at this time of night. The electricity is very expensive here.

YOSHI: I see. But, I don't know what kind of arrangements you have with the school. I naturally assumed that I would be able to study, using the light, as much as I wanted.

LANDLADY: Unfortunately, that is not my understanding. Anyway, you have a study room in the school. Why don't you study there?

YOSHI: I do use it, but it closes at 9 p.m.

LANDLADY: Well, if you work that much you should be tired. You should be resting here.

YOSHI: That's not what I'm here for, I'm afraid. I have taken a year off from the university in Tokyo. All of my friends are studying very hard back home. I am vying with them and can't waste a second here.

LANDLADY: But, I can't let you use it. It's costing us a lot. I've got to turn off the light.

YOSHI: What are you doing? Look, I'm not some sort of hanger-on or something. According to the school brochure, I should be treated like a resident-guest. You are really getting on my nerves.

LANDLADY: So are you.

YOSHI: Right. Let's have a compromise then. As I have to work late at night in the room, I'll pay you directly for the electricity which is not covered by the school. How about that?

LANDLADY: If you say so, that might work.

(One) ~ *haitte kulu*: ~ comes in. *te* form + *kimasu*; indicates that something/someone is coming towards the speaker.

(Two) ~ *itadaite inai*: ~ are not given ~. *te* form + *imasu/masen* (negative), expresses the present progressive tense, a habitual action or a state of being.

(Three) ~ *sasete itadakelu* ~: ~ will be given the opportunity to do ~. *Itadakimasu* is the humble form of *molaimasu*. *te* form + *molaimasu*; receiving someone's favour, tangible or intangible.

(Four) ~ *tsukawanai no?*: ~ don't you use ~? Plain (*nai*) form + *no?*; in casual speech *no* is used as a question marker rather than *ka*.

(Five) ~ *ilu hazu desu*: ~ supposed to be ~. Plain form + *hazu desu*; expressing supposition.

(Six.) ~ *tsukawaselalenai* ~: ~ can't let someone use something , a causative passive negative form.

(Seven) *Chō mukatsuku na!*: It's really infuriating! This is a contemporary expression that is impolite but used commonly among young people.

● *Nalita Kūkō de: At Nalita Airport*

Shin Tōkyō Kokusai Kūkō dewa, ōzei no hito ga yuki katte imasu. Sotsugyō go, jūnen tatte, hutali no josei ga gūzen kūkō de saikaishimasu..

MIYUKI: *Sumimasen, Kaneko Tomomi-san jā alimasen ka? Oboete imasu? Kawata Miyuki desu. Jū-nen mae daigaku de issho datta.*

TOMOMI: *Uwa! Kigū da wa ne. O-aisulu nante, odoloita wa. O-genki?*

MIYUKI: *Okage de genki ni yattelu wa. Tomomi-san wa dō?*

TOMOMI: *Sotsugyō shite sugu Amelikajin to kekkon shita no yo. Kale asoko ni kodomo-tachi to ilu wa. Yonin kodomo ga ilu no.*

MIYUKI: *Sugoi wa ne! Yonin mo! Dakedo kale hansamu ne. Yatta janai. Kale Amelika no doko no shusshin?*

TOMOMI: *Boston yo. Kole kala Boston ni iku no. Tokolode, Kawata-san wa dochila e?*

MIYUKI: *Junēbu ni yuku no. O-yasumi o mukō de sugosō to omotte.*

TOMOMI: *O-hitoli? Saiai no go-shujin wa dōshita no?*

MIYUKI: *Kale, Shingapōlu de shigoto nano yo. Shigoto no ato, chokusetsu Junēbu e kulu koto ni natte ilu no.*

TOMOMI: *Go-shujin o-isogashii no ne. A, mōikanakucha. Minna mattelu wa. Meishi ka nanika mottelu?*

MIYUKI: *Chotto matte. Kole ga watashi no denwa-bangō yo. Nihon ni kaettala denwa chōdai, o-aishitai wa.*

TOMOMI: *Ii wa ne! Tanoshimi ni shitelu wa.*

MIYUKI: *Watashi mo yo. Sole jā, itte lasshai.*

TOMOMI: *Aligatō.*

At the Tokyo International Airport of Nalita, there are lots of people coming and going. Two ladies bump into each other, ten years after their graduation.

MIYUKI: Excuse me! Am I right in thinking that you are Miss

	Tomomi Kaneko? Remember me? I am Miyuki Kawata. I was with you at college ten years ago.
TOMOMI:	Gosh! What a coincidence! Fancy seeing you here. How are you keeping?
MIYUKI:	No major grumbles, actually. How are things with you?
TOMOMI:	As a matter of fact, I married an American right after graduation. He's over there with our kids. We have four.
MIYUKI:	Goodness gracious! Four kids! But your husband is good looking, isn't he? Aren't you lucky. Where in America is he from ?
TOMOMI:	He's originally from Boston. That's where we are heading right now. But tell me, what brings you here?
MIYUKI:	I'm taking a flight to Geneva; I'm going to spend my holidays there.
TOMOMI:	All alone? What happened to your beloved husband?
MIYUKI:	He's got some business to attend to in Singapore, so he'll be flying directly from there to Geneva.
TOMOMI:	What a flyer he is! Good gracious! I've got to go, I'm afraid. They are waiting for me. Do you have a card of some kind?
MIYUKI:	Just a sec. This is my telephone number. Why don't you give me a ring when you return to Japan so that we can get together?
TOMOMI:	That sounds great! I look forward to that.
MIYUKI:	So do I. Have a nice flight then.
TOMOMI:	The same to you.

(One) ~ yuki (iki) katte imasu: ~ are coming and going. te form + imasu; a habitual action or a state of being.

(Two) ~ datta: ~ was ~. ta form: the plain form of deshita.

(Three) ~ da wa ne: ~ isn't it, a feminine sentence ending; desu ne is the common form and is used by both genders.

(Four) O-genki?: A familiar way of saying 'O-genki desu ka?'

(Five) ~ no yo: A feminine sentence ending.

(Six) Yatta janai: Well done, a familiar way of saying 'yalimashita ne'.

(Seven) ~ omotte ~ : ~ am (are, is) thinking of ~, '~ omotte ilu no' is a proper form of saying this.

(Eight) ~ *ikanakucha:* ~ must go, a familiar way of saying '*ikanakeleba-nali-masen*'.

(Nine) ~ *mottelu?:* Do you have ~ ? The more polite way of putting it is '*Motte imasu ka?*'

(Ten)~ *chōdai:* Please give me ~, '*kudasai*' is a polite form of this.

● *Hotelu ni te: In a Hotel*

The two persons featured in this dialogue are Mr Yoshikata Kawata (YK) and the assistant manager (*Ashisutanto manēja* – AM) of the hotel.

YK: *Moshi, moshi.*
AM: *Lesepushon desu.*
YK: *Gō san nana (537) no mono desu ga.*
AM: *Kawata-san desu ne.*
YK: *Sō desu. Heya no chekku-auto no jikan ni tsuite o-tazune shitai no desu ga.*
AM: *Hu hum.*
YK: *Shōgo made ni chekku-auto sulu tsumoli datta no desu ga, saki hodo chōshoku no toki ni Tan-san to iu josei no kata to o-hanashi-shitala.*
AM: *Hu hum.*
YK: *Go-shinsetsu ni, watashi ga Shingapōlu ni shūjitsu ilu to ittala, chekku-auto no jikan o gogo sanji ni shite kudasatta no desu.*
AM: *Hu hum.*
YK: *Sono koto ni tsuite o-kiki shiyō to omotte denwa-shita no desu.*
AM: *Hu hum. Ē, Kawata-san. Sanji made o-tsukai ni nalemasu.*
YK: *Sole wa yokatta. Tokolo de, anata no o-namae wa?*
AM: *Rajab desu.*
YK: *Dono-yō ni kaku no desu ka?*
AM: *R-A-J-A-B to kakimasu.*
YK: *Sōsulu to, Rajabu-san desu ne?*
AM: *Hu hum.*
YK: *Rajabu-san, saki hodo kala watashi ni taishite, kodomo ka, kakyu no iyashii mono ni demo hanashite ilu yōna sono 'hu hum' to iu taido wa dō-iu koto na no desu ka?*
AM: *Ie, sō dewa nai no desu. Moshi sono yōna inshō o o-mochi ni natta no nala, makoto ni mōshiwakealimasen.*
YK: *Chotto baka ni shitelu no dewa nai desu ka?*
AM: *Gokai da to omoimasu yo, Kawata-san.*

YK: *Rajabu-san de shita yo ne.*
AM: *Sayō de gozaimasu.*
YK: *Nihonjin wa tashika ni Eigo o hanasu no wa umaku nai kamo shile-masen. Shikashi, dakala to itte anata yoli ototte ilu to iu koto ni wa nalanai deshō. Anata ga Nihonjin yoli shōshō Eigo ga umai kala to itte anata no hōga Nihonjin yoli sugulete ilu to iu koto ni wa nalanai no dewa nai no desu ka?*
AM: *O-sshalu tōli desu.*
YK: *Saki hodo no yōna taido wa kole kala kesshite totte hoshiku nai desu ne. Moshi kole kala mo sono yōna taido o o-toli ni naleba, o-taku no hotelu ni shukuhaku-sulu Nihonjin wa inakunalu to omoimasu yo. Yoloshii desu ka? Kokolo shite oite kudasai, Rajabu-san.*
AM: *Kashikomalimashita. Kichō-na kyōkun o itadaki hontō ni aligatō goza-imashita.*
YK: *O-wakali itadakemashita ka. Sankō ni shite itadakeleba saiwai desu.*
AM: *Taihen sankō ni nalimashita. Aligatō gozaimashita.*

YK: Hello.
AM: Reception.
YK: I'm in room 537.
HM: You are Mr Kawata.
YK: Right. I would like to inquire about my checking-out time.
AM: Uh-hmm.
YK: I was to check out by noon, however when I went down for breakfast I had a word with one of your colleagues, a Ms Tan.
AM: Uh-hmm.
YK: She kindly suggested that I could keep my room until 3 p.m. rather than 12 noon, as I will be spending the whole day in Singapore.
AM: Uh-hmm.
YK: I would like to confirm if this message has been passed on to you.
AM: Uh-hmm. Yes, Mr Kawata, you can keep your room until 3 p.m.
YK: That's good. By the way, may I have your name, please?
AM: Rajab.
YK: How would you spell that, please?
AM: It's spelt R-A-J-A-B.
YK: So, it's Mr Rajab?
AM: Uh-hmm.
YK: Mr Rajab, what do you mean when you always say 'Uh-hmm' – as if you were talking to a child, or someone inferior.

AM: No, Sir. If I have given you that impression, I'm very sorry, Sir.

YK: Look! I wasn't born yesterday, Mr Rajab. You can't make a fool out of me.

AM: Mr Kawata, you are misunderstanding me.

YK: Mr Rajab.

AM: Yes, sir.

YK: My, compatriots, the Japanese, might not be linguistically talented, but it doesn't mean that we are inferior to you, or you are superior to us simply because you speak slightly better English than we do.

AM: Of course, sir.

YK: Will you never take that attitude to the Japanese again? If you keep on doing it you will pay for it as you will have no more Japanese customers, I'm afraid. Have I made myself clear to you, Mr Rajab?

AM: Yes, sir. Thank you very much for your valuable lesson, Mr Kawata.

YK: Not at all, Mr Rajab. A good day to you.

AM: The same to you, sir.

(One) ~ o tazune shitai ~ : ~ would like to ask ~ . o+ stem + shimasu; an honorific form showing humbleness. Stem + taidesu; would like to do something.

(Two) ~ o-hanashi-shitala: After speaking ~, an action verb noun. ta form + la; if, when, a conditional form.

(Three) ~ kudasatta ~: ~ gave me ~, a humble form of kulelu (to give).

(Four) ~ o-kiki shiyō ~: ~ will ask ~, o + stem + shimasu; showing humbleness.

(Five) ~ o-tsukai ni nalemasu: ~ can use ~ , o + stem + ni nalemasu; an honorific form demonstrating respect or humbleness.

(Six) ~ o-mochi ni natta no nala: If you had ~, again an honorific form.

(Seven) ~ yo ne: ~ wasn't it, a sentence ending form used to convey the speaker's request for agreement or confirmation.

(Eight) ~ nalanai deshō: ~ won't be ~. Plain (nai) form + deshō; emphasising one's impression.

(Nine) ~ totte hoshikunai ~ : ~ don't want somebody to do something, te form + hoshikunai ~.

(Ten) ~ o o-toli ni naleba: If you keep on (doing) ~, behaving in such a manner, conditional form.

● *Nihon de Eigo wa manabelu no ka?: Can one learn English in Japan?*

This discussion involves the Teacher and his four students Masahito Watanabe, Tatsuya Hasegawa, Yukiko Yokozuka and Hideko Terada.

TEACHER: *Kyō minasan to hanashi aitai koto wa, 'Nihon de Eigo wa manabelu no ka?' to iu koto desu. Donata ka go-iken wa alimasen ka?*

MASAHITO: *Kyō no londai to chokusetsu kankei aluka dō ka wakalanai no desu ga, telebi de yatte ilu 'Eigo-gakkō no kōkōku wa chotto okashii no jyā nai ka?' to zutto omotteita no desu ga.*

TEACHER: *Sole wa ii tokolo ni kigatsukimashita ne. Kaleno Eigo wa, watashi ga minasan ni itsumo hanashite ilu, 'Nihongo-Eigo' desu ne, yōsulu ni Nihonjin to ichibu no Ajiajin ni shika wakkatte molaenai Eigo desu.*

TATSUYA: *Sole wa dō-iu koto desu ka? Nihonjin ni likai-salelu to iu no wa wakalu no desu ga. Ajia no hito-tachi nimo wakkatte molaelu no desu ka?*

TEACHER: *Hai. Gengo no oto to iu kanten kala sulu to, ikutsu-ka no Ajia no gengo wa Nihongo ni niteilu mono mo alu kala desu. Mata, Nihongo ni wa Eigo no ikutsu-ka no kihonteki-na oto ga nakute, solela no oto nashi de Eigo o hanashiteilu, aluiwa hanashiteilu to omotte ilu Nihonjin no 'Nihongo-Eigo' ni nalasalete ilu Ōbeijin nimo aluteido wakalu yō desu.*

YUKIKO: *Nihongo ni nai 'Eigo no kihonteki-na oto' to iu no wa, watashi-tachi ga jugyōchū ni kulikaeshi kulikaeshi lenshū saselalelu, 'F, L, R, V' to itta yōna oto desu ka?*

TEACHER: *Sono tōli desu. Solela no oto nashi dewa, anata no Eigo wa sekaijū doko e itte mo wakkatte molaelu koto ni wa nalimasen. Toku ni Eigo o bokokugo to shite ilu, Eikoku, Sukottolando, Ailulando, Uēluzu, Amelika, Ōsutolalia, Nyūjīlando toitta tokolo dewa hotondo tsūji nai to omoimasu.*

YUKIKO: *Sole wa gyaku ni solela no oto (Nihon no gakkō dewa naka naka manabe nai) o shūtoku sae suleba, tatoeba Eikoku e itte mo watashi no Eigo wa tsūjilu to iu koto desu yo ne.*

TEACHER: Mochilon desu. Jitsu wa sono koto de watashi ni wa Eikoku de
             'nigai omoide' ga alimasu.

HIDEKO: Sashisawali nakeleba sono 'nigai omoide' o o-hanashi itadake-
             masen ka.

TEACHER: Sō desu ne. Sole wa watashi ga hajimete Eikoku e itta 1973
             (sen kyūhyaku nanajyū san) nen no koto desu. Watashi wa
             London no Bikutolia-eki (Victoria Station) de 'Ramsgate' to iu
             tokolo e iku no de kippu o kau tokolo deshita.

HIDEKO: Sono toki wa Eigo wa sudeni o-jōzu datte no desu ka.

TEACHER: Ima sono koto o o-hanashi itashimasu. Jissai no tokolo, watashi
             wa Eigo wa mattaku sono jiten dewa hanasenakatta to itta
             hōga yoi to omoimasu.

MASAHITO: Naze desu ka.

TEACHER: Jitsu wa watashi no Eikoku Iyūgaku no o-sewa o shite kudasatta
             sensei ga, 'Kawata-kun Eigo no walui kuse ga tsuku to ikenai
             kala Nihon dewa Eigo o benkyō shite ikanai hōga ii yo' to o-
             sshatta kala desu.

TATSUYA: Sono kolo Tōkyō niwa Eigo no gakkōwa nakatta no desu ka.

TEACHER: Sono sensei no o-hanashi dewa, 'hontō no Eigo' o o-shiete kulelu
             gakkō wa tōji Tōkyō ni wa nai to iu koto deshita. Sonna wake
             de watashi wa, mattaku eikaiwa no benkyō o sezuni Eikoku ni
             itta no desu.

HIDEKO: Sole wa taihen datta deshō ne. Sensei no nigai omoide o
             tsuzukete itadakemasen ka. Sensei wa tashika Bikutolia-eki
             (Victoria Station) de. . .

TEACHER: Sō deshita ne. Watashi wa kippu uliba ni itte, tenkeiteki-na
             'Nihongo Eigo' de 'Lamuzugēto made ichimai kudasai' to
             iimashita. Kippu uliba no ekiin-san wa kyoton to shita kao o
             shite, 'doko e yukitai no desu ka' to kulikaeshi kulikaeshi kiki
             kaeshite kimashita. To iu no wa watashi ga 'Ramsgate' dewa
             naku te 'Lamuzugēto' to hatsuon-shite ita kala desu.

YUKIKO: 'Ramsgate' to ienakatta no desu ka. 'R' no hatsuon ga
             dekinakatta to iu koto desu ka.

TEACHER: Hai. Anata mitai ni dekileba yokatta no desu ga. Gohun gulai
             soko de 'Lamuzugēto' to itte ita no deshō ka. Kigatsuite milu to
             watashi no ushilo ni wa nagai letsu ga dekite imashita. Totemo
             hazukashikatta node, saigo ni wa, 'Lamuzugēto kudasai' to
             donatte shimaimashita.

MASAHITO: Ekiin-san wa odoloita deshō ne. Kale no hannō wa dō deshita
             ka.

TEACHER: Sono toki made ni wa kale mo, 'Lamuzugēto' no oto ni ichi-ban chikai oto no eki wa 'Ramsgate' dakala kitto kono tōyōjin wa 'Ramsgate' ni ikitai no dakala 'Ramsgate' no kippu o yalō to iu ketsulon ni ttashiteita no deshō. Yatto no koto de 'Ramsgate' e no kippu o teniilelu koto ga dekimashita. Ōgesa ni itte ilu to omowalelu kamo shilemasen ga keshite sonna koto wa alimasen.

HIDEKO: Sono toki no sensei no o-kao ga mitakatta desu wa. Sono ekiin-san wa, sensei o kalakatta no dewa nai deshō ka. Eikokujin wa toki toshite gaikokujin ni henken o motte ilu to kiita koto ga alimasu.

TEACHER: Sōiu hito mo ilu kamo shilemasen ga, keshite subete no Eikokujin ga hushinsetsu de alu to iu koto dewa alimasen. Sono ekiin wa, chotto talinakatta kamo shilemasen ga, dōji ni kale to shite wa saidaigen no dolyoku o shite 'Lamuzugēto' to iu chimei no eki o sagashiteita no kamo shilemasen. Shikashi dō-shite mo omoitsukanakkatta node, 'mō ichido o-negai shimasu' to kulikaeshita no deshō.

TATSUYA: Ekiin-san mo taihen datta no desu ne. Kale wa taihen hungai-shiteita deshō ne.

TEACHER: Watashi wa motto hungai-shiteita to omoimasu yo. Izule ni shite mo, watashi no kono 'nigai keiken' ga monogatatte ilu yōni. Eigo wa 'shikaku-gengo de alu Nihongo' ni kulabete totemo 'onsei-gengo teki' de alu to iu koto desu.

YUKIKO: Mō sukoshi sono koto o kuwashiku go-setsumei itadakemasen ka.

TEACHER: Nihongo wa, tatoeba '大 dai' (big) to iu ji o lei ni tolu to, ten o mannaka ni utsu to '太 hutoi' (thick) to iu ji ni nali, mata 'dai' no ji no naname ueni ten o uteba '犬 inu' (dog) ni nalimasu. Kono yōni Nihongo wa, shikaku ni ōkiku izon-sulu gengo de alu to iu koto desu.

HIDEKO: To iu koto wa, sensei wa shikakuteki ni goku no imi o kaelu koto ga dekilu node Nihongo wa Shikaku-gengo da to o-sshalu no desu ne.

TEACHER: Sono tōli desu. Mochilon kono koto wa tsune-ni hutatsu no gengo o hikaku shita toki ni ielu koto desu. Eigo to Nihongo o hikaku shita toki, watashi wa Eigo wa onsei-gengo de ali, Nihongo wa shikaku-gengo de alu to ielu to omoimasu.

TATSUYA: Kole de walewale ga kulikaeshi Nihongo ni nai 'Eigo no oto' o lenshū shinakeleba nalanai wade ga wakatta yōna kigashimasu. 'Kole kala wa kokolo o ilekaelu zo.'

TEACHER: *Watashi ga iou to shiteilu koto ga wakatte itadakete totemo
              uleshii desu.*
MASAHITO: *Yōshi. Boku wa Nihongo ni nai Eigo no oto o kanalazu shūtoku-
              sulu zo. Solela no oto nashi dewa Nihonjin ni shika tsūjinai
              'telebi no otoko no hito' no Eigo ni natte shimaimasu kala ne.
              'Sekai de tsūyō sulu Eigo' ni nalu yōni gambalimasu.*
TEACHER: *Sono chōshi de gambatte kudasai. Sō desu ne, kole de 'Nihon
              de Eigo wa manabelu no ka?' to iu londai ni taisulu hitotsu no
              kotae ga deta yō desu ne. Tsumali, Kawata-shiki de Eigo o
              benkyō-suleba minasan no Eigo wa sekaijyū doko e itte mo
              daijōbu da to iu koto desu. Hanashiai ni sanka-shite itadaite
              aligatō gozaimashita.*
EVERYONE: *Dōitashimashite.*

TEACHER: The topic that we are to discuss here is, 'Can one learn
              English in Japan?' Anyone?
MASAHITO: Well, I don't know if what I'm going to say is directly
              related to the topic, however, I have always wondered if
              the person of that famous language school is speaking
              English properly in the advertisement.
TEACHER: Actually, that's a good point. His English is what I call
              'Japlish', which can only be understood amongst the
              Japanese and by some Asian people.
TATSUYA: What do you mean by that? I know that the Japanese can
              understand it, but could it be understood by some Asian
              people as well?
TEACHER: Yes, it could be. Because, I think, sound-wise some Asian
              languages are similar to the Japanese language. It could
              also be understood even by some Europeans, or
              Americans for that matter, who have been in Japan for
              long enough to get used to this Japanese-English, 'Japlish',
              which lacks some of the essential sounds in English.
YUKIKO: Are those the sounds, 'F, L, R, V' and all that, which we
              repeatedly practise in our class?
TEACHER: That's spot-on. Without them your English is not going to
              be understood worldwide, particularly in countries where
              English is spoken as the first language such as England,
              Scotland, Ireland, Wales, the United States of America,
              Australia, New Zealand, and some others.
YUKIKO: Does this mean that if I gain those sounds of English –

which are not being taught at school in Japan, I can get myself understood, for instance, in England?

TEACHER: Definitely. If you've really acquired them, that is. Actually, that reminds me of my own experience in England.

HIDEKO: What sort of experience was it, if I may ask, please?

TEACHER: Well, it was back in 1973, when I first went over to England. I was at Victoria Station in London where I was to get a train ticket for a place called Ramsgate.

HIDEKO: Did you speak English well then?

TEACHER: I was just about to come to that. To answer your question frankly: no I did not. Actually, to be more precise, I would say that my English was almost non-existent at that time.

MASAHITO: Why was that?

TEACHER: Because my professor at my university in Tokyo, who kindly arranged for me to go over to England, advised me strongly not to study English in Japan as I might pick up 'some bad habits of speaking English'.

TATSUYA: Were there any English language schools in Tokyo then?

TEACHER: According to him, there was no English school around in Tokyo those days where one could learn proper English. So, I studied no conversational English at all before going to England.

HIDEKO: That's really very interesting, I must say. But, may I urge you to continue relating your experience, please. You were at Victoria Station, I think?

TEACHER: That's right. I went to the ticket office and said with a typical Japanese accent, 'I want a ticket for Lamsgate, please.' The man on the other side of the counter looked perplexed and kept asking where I wanted to go by saying 'Sorry?' as I kept on saying 'Lamsgate' for Ramsgate.

YUKIKO: So you were unable to say 'Ramsgate' properly because you could not pronounce the 'R'.

TEACHER: Yes – unlike you. After five minutes, or so, of repeating 'Lamsgate' for Ramsgate, I realised that there was a long queue behind me. I became rather embarrassed, so I could not help shouting at him,' Lamsgate, please.'

MASAHITO: Did he get surprised? What was his reaction to your shouting?

TEACHER: By then he must have come to the conclusion that the closest sounding place to 'Lamsgate', which I kept repeating, was in fact Ramsgate. 'So give him a ticket for

Ramsgate.' Thank God! Eventually, I got a ticket for Ramsgate – cross my heart – I'm not exaggerating the incident at all.

HIDEKO: I should have been there! I don't know if he was trying to make a fool out of you; the English are sometimes prejudiced against foreign people, I hear.

TEACHER: Well some of them might be, but not all of them. The ticket clerk might have been a little thick, however, equally he might have been making a great effort to locate a place called 'Lamsgate', but he couldn't find one, therefore he kept on saying 'Sorry?' repeatedly.

TATSUYA: Poor chap! He must have been indignant with you, I suppose.

TEACHER: I was more than that. Anyway, my experience does illustrate well, I think, how vocal English is as compared to the Japanese language, which is a visual one.

YUKIKO: Would you elaborate on that, please ?

TEACHER: The Japanese language is a visual one in the sense that, for instance, this Japanese character '大 dai' means big in English. By adding a dot in the middle of it ' 太 hutoi' – the character changes its meaning, now it means thick. More still, if you put a dot above the character on its right hand side ' 犬 inu', it is now dog in English. Now that I've said this, you hopefully get my point.

HIDEKO: Am I right in saying that the Japanese language is visual as it distinguishes the meaning of one character from another by the sense of vision?

TEACHER: Brilliant! Albeit it's always a comparison, in the case of English and Japanese when one compares them, English is a vocal language whereas Japanese is a visual one.

TATSUYA: Now, I'm beginning to realise why we have to spend so much time in practising certain English sounds! I've got to turn over a new leaf!

TEACHER: I'm delighted to know that you are beginning to appreciate the core of my teaching method.

MASAHITO: Right. So, I have to get myself fully acquainted with those English sounds which we don't have in our language. Without them, my English will be the same as that of the character on the TV commercial, which can only be understood by the Japanese. I must work harder on those sounds to get myself understood world-wide in English.

TEACHER: You have hit the nail right on the head! Well, that leads to
             one conclusion to this topic of 'Can one learn English in
             Japan?' Yes, one certainly can – so long as one learns
             English with the Kawata Method of Learning English
             Conversation. I would like to thank you all for partici-
             pating in this discussion.
EVERYONE: Not at all.

(One) ~ *alu ka dō ka* ~ : If there is, or not. Plain form + *ka dō ka*; whether
or not.

(Two) ~ *omotte-ita* ~: ~ was thinking ~. ~ *tteita*; ~ was/were ~ ing, past
continuous.

(Three) ~ *nalasalete* ~ : ~ was made accustomed to ~; a passive form.

(Four) ~ *saselalelu* ~: ~ made to do ~, causative passive 1.

(Five) ~ *wakatte molaelu* ~: ~ was understood, *te* form + *molaimasu*;
receiving someone's favour.

(Six) ~ *nakeleba*: if it is not ~, ~ *ba*; conditional.

(Seven) ~ *hanasenakatta*: ~ could not speak; plain form past negative.

(Eight) ~ *nakatta*: There was not ~, plain form past negative; dictionary
form 'alu'.

(Nine) ~ *oshiete kulelu* ~: to teach someone something. *te* form + *kulemasu*; someone does me, or us, a favour.

(Ten) '~ *yukitai no desu*' is a formal way of saying '*yukitain desu*'; ~ would
like to go. Stem + *tai (no) desu*; would like to do something, expressing
the speaker's desire.

(Eleven) ~ *hatsuon-shite ita*: ~ used to pronounce ~. *te* form + *ita
(imashita)*: a habitual action or a state of being.

(Twelve) ~ *itte ita*: ~ used to say. *te* form + *ita (imashita)*; a state of being.

(Thirteen) ~ *donatte shimaimashita*: ~ was oblidged to shout. *te* form +
shimaimashita; indicates that something has been completely finished, it
also expresses the speaker's regret in doing something.

(Fourteen) '~ *mita katta*' is a shorter form of '*mitai to omotta*': ~ wanted
to see. Stem + *tai desu*; expresses the speaker's desire.

(Fifteen) ~ *kiita koto ga alimasu:* ~ have heard of it. *ta* form + *koto ga alimasu*; to have experienced something.

(Sixteen) ~ *hungai-shite ita deshō:* ~ must have been indignant. *hungai-sulu*; an action noun verb, meaning to be indignant. *te* form + *imasu* + *deshō*; a state of being + emphasising one's impression.

(Seventeen) ~ *monogatatte ilu ~:* ~ to illustrate well. *te* form + *imasu (ilu)*; a state of being.

(Eighteen) ~ *ni izon-sulu:* to depend on, an action noun verb.

(Nineteen) *o-sshalu:* an honorific form of *iu* (to say).

(Twenty) ~ *hikaku-shite:* ~ compared. *hikaku-sulu*; to compare, an action noun verb.

(Twenty-one) ~ *shinakeleba nalimasen:* ~ must do ~. *nai* form: *nakeleba nalimasen*.

(Twenty-two) ~ *kiga-shimasu:* ~ think (to feel). *kiga-sulu*; to think (to feel), an action noun verb.

(Twenty-three) ~ *wakatte itadakete ~:* as ~ understood ~. The *te* form itself is often used as a connective. It is also used to show the order in which actions occur consecutively; 'and then'.

(Twenty-four) *Shūtoku-sulu:* to master, an action noun verb.

(Twenty-five) ~ *natte shimaimasu:* ~ would become ~. *te* form + *shimaimasu*; expresses the speaker's regret in doing something.

(Twenty-six) ~ *benkyō-suleba:* if (subject) study, ~ *ba* ; conditional. *benkyō-sulu*; to study.

(Twenty-seven) ~ *sanka-shite itadaite:* ~ participating in ~. *te* form + *molaimasu*; receiving somebody's favour. *'Itadakimasu'* is the honorific form of *'molaimasu'*.

Postscript

THE OFFICIAL NAME of the country known as '*Igilis*' in Japanese is 'The United Kingdom of Great Britain and Northern Ireland'. The three countries in Great Britain – namely England, Scotland and Wales – were united by a king and together with the Northern Ireland Province became the United Kingdom, presently reigned over by Queen Elizabeth II.

The reason it is called '*Igilis*' in Japanese is because during the Edo Period (1603-1867) '*Ingles*' in Portugese and '*Engles*' in Dutch were used to mean English. '*Igilis*' is the Japanese pronunciation of the Dutch and Portugese words for English and not a word that derives directly from the English language. So, '*Igilis*' means 'English' and does not include Scotland, Wales and Northern Ireland. Therefore '*Igilis*' in Japanese is an inadequate word for the United Kingdom of Great Britain and Northern Ireland.

The peoples of Scotland, Wales and Northern Ireland have pride in their culture and history. Especially James VI of Scotland who united Scotland with England and made the first Union Jack Flag in 1606. The pride of Scottish people will be hurt very much if you call them '*Igilis*' (English).

I therefore maintain that '*Igilis*' in Japanese, presently used for the United Kingdom of Great Britain and Northern Ireland should be changed to Britain ('*Bliten*' in Japanese) and its people to British ('*Blitish*' in Japanese).

I mentioned this because I am trying to teach the Japanese reader the English being spoken in England. They have their own languages in Scotland, Ireland and Wales which are actually being spoken by an increasing smaller number of people these days. Although they use English as their offical language, their English is different from English (Standard English).

In this book, I have been advocating that because of different racial backgrounds, English and Japanese have different linguistic characteristics.

Originally, the English were nomads in the continent of Europe, moving from one place to another, verbally and skilfully establishing good human relations with the people wherever they went, and they became very good at diplomacy. English has therefore become a vocal language and developed more complicated sounds and a wider tonal range than Japanese, distinguishing meanings of words by sound or by intonation (ban-van, law-raw, etc.).

On the other hand, the Japanese have been always engaged in agriculture, and have lived in small communities; they are islanders who have always been isolated from the rest of the world. They tried to speak as little as possible so as not to be ousted 'Mulahachibu' from their villages. Consequently, Japanese has become a language which is relatively poor in sounds.

For English people, it is not enough that they can read and write English, 'it is meaningless, if they can't speak English'. So when a Japanese person tries to learn English, he or she must first appreciate the importance of verbal communication, that he/she has to be able to speak English. And in order to be able to speak English he/she has to start acquiring those sounds of English which do not exist in Japanese.

Amongst those sounds, 'the actual sound of R as it is heard in words' is the most important of them all. I have clearly indicated how this sound should be pronounced in this book. If a Japanese person acquires this sound, he or she will undoubtedly be able to speak English. And as Japanese is a monotonous, flat language, the Japanese have the potential to be able to speak any foreign language well, including English. Therefore, I would like the Japanese reader to become aware that the Japanese have a head start in learning English!

In Chapter Eight, many aspects of the Japanese language are discussed; amongst them it is pointed out that although there is no such sound R (the actual sound of R as it is heard in words) in Japanese, R was used in the Hepburn System of Romanized script some 140 years ago and it is still being used in Japan. The author maintains that R should never have been used in the first place in the Hepburn System as it creates many misunderstandings, one of which is to greatly confuse Japanese language learners when they see 'Rondon' or 'rampu' written with 'R' in their text books, but they are actually 'London' or 'lamp' respectively in English. For this very reason, in the Kawata System of Romanized script, 'la, li, lu, le, lo, lya, lyu and lyo' are used, instead of 'ra, ri, ru, re, ro, rya, ryu and ryo' in the Hepburn System of Romanized script.

Having been acquainted with the Japanese national character, the Japanese language and above all the method of pronouncing 'the actual sound of R as it is heard in words', you are now qualified as being able to teach English to the Japanese.

I hope, most sincerely, that you will be successful in the career of teaching English, or at whatever you do in the future.